'Bernie Bulkin distils decades of experience into his lively analysis of causes of start-up failure, many of which resonate with me. Entrepreneurs and investors will find his discussion of strategy and behavioural economics particularly valuable... if they take the time to read, digest and practise the lessons in there.'

Dr Hermann Hauser FRS, KBE, Amadeus Capital Partners

'*Why Start-Ups Fail* is enormously relevant to all involved in start-ups. These are wise words to steer you through perilous waters, identifying six main, and avoidable, causes of failure. His analysis of the skills and competences required of leaders is essential reading, alongside the focus on securing an effective focused board involving people with diverse experience. Concise, relevant and beautifully written; yet again, Bernie Bulkin has produced an accessible volume that all should read.'

Baroness Virginia Bottomley, Chair, Board Practice, Odgers

'Bernie Bulkin reframes the venture-capital mindset with the precision of a scientist and the empathy of a mentor. *Why Start-Ups Fail* isn't about postmortems; it's about pattern recognition – how to turn the most common traps of technology, money, and ego into opportunities for growth and resilience. He shows how the start-up world's "culture of failure" is not destiny but a design flaw. This book belongs in every accelerator, boardroom, and MBA syllabus concerned with building businesses that actually last.'

Joel Makower, Co-Founder and Chair, Trellis Group

'If you are starting a business and put this book back on the shelf without reading it, your chances of failure just went up. Be smart – read it and act on it. There is a lifetime's wisdom here written just for you.'

Fred Brown, Partner, Kindred Group

'Essential reading for those passionate, energetic types driven to lead, invest in or oversee start-ups and early-stage businesses. Bernie Bulkin has distilled a lifetime of experience into a highly readable text packed with sage advice.'

Ian Simm, Founder & CEO, Impax Asset Management Group plc

'Bernie weaves a great deal of experience into each powerful set of lessons. He analyses some really eye-opening failures, to help investors and start-ups avoid doing it again! I'm buying my whole team their own copies.'

Cam Ross, CEO, Green Angel Ventures

'From a founder and VC perspective, I believe Bernie Bulkin captures what most founders learn only after painful experience and what most investors never learn at all. *Why Start-Ups Fail* is a powerful guide for anyone determined to create real, lasting value and increase the odds of real success.'

William Chen, Co-Founder of Billpoint,
Founding Managing Partner, ClearVue Partners

'Must read for budding entrepreneurs as well as grizzled investors – with deep insights and pragmatic advice to accelerate success and make failure an exception.'

Atul Arya, Chief Energy Strategist, S&P Global

'Bernie's wealth of experience shines through clearly. He delivers a number of gems, including "you should spend very little of your effort on the size of the market, and a lot of it on the structure of the market", making the book a great read for thoughtful founders and investors.'

Patrick Sheehan, Founder and Managing Partner, ETF Partners,
The Environmental Technologies Fund

'For anyone entering the start-up world, this book is a must-read foundation course – compiling decades of learnings into a very accessible and valuable guidebook. Most start-up writing focuses on the heroic success stories. Bernie, instead, critically examines what makes companies fail. Knowing what to avoid, knowing what to challenge and knowing where the failure points are will vastly improve the probability of success for companies and their investors. This is required reading for founders, executives and investors.'

Alan Barton, Board Member of Wilbur-Ellis Holdings,
Chairman of Nuritas Ltd, and Senior Advisor to Natrium Capital

'Bernie Bulkin brings the wisdom of his vast experience in highlighting the main causes for start-up failure and how to avoid them. A book every founder and venture investor needs to read.'

Lord Barker of Battle

WHY START-UPS FAIL
Avoiding the traps on the path to commercial success

BERNIE BULKIN

BLOOMSBURY BUSINESS
LONDON • NEW YORK • OXFORD • NEW DELHI • SYDNEY

BLOOMSBURY BUSINESS
Bloomsbury Publishing Plc, 50 Bedford Square, London, WC1B 3DP, UK
Bloomsbury Publishing Inc, 1359 Broadway, New York, NY 10018, USA
Bloomsbury Publishing Ireland, 29 Earlsfort Terrace, Dublin 2, D02 AY28, Ireland

BLOOMSBURY, BLOOMSBURY BUSINESS and the Diana logo are trademarks of
Bloomsbury Publishing Plc

First published in Great Britain 2026

Copyright © Bernie Bulkin, 2026

Bernie Bulkin has asserted his right under the Copyright, Designs and Patents Act, 1988,
to be identified as Author of this work.

For legal purposes the Acknowledgements on p. xi constitute an extension
of this copyright page.

Cover design: Louise Dugdale

All rights reserved. No part of this publication may be: i) reproduced or transmitted in any form, electronic or mechanical, including photocopying, recording or by means of any information storage or retrieval system without prior permission in writing from the publishers; or ii) used or reproduced in any way for the training, development or operation of artificial intelligence (AI) technologies, including generative AI technologies. The rights holders expressly reserve this publication from the text and data mining exception as per Article 4(3) of the Digital Single Market Directive (EU) 2019/790.

Bloomsbury Publishing Plc does not have any control over, or responsibility for, any third-party websites referred to or in this book. All internet addresses given in this book were correct at the time of going to press. The author and publisher regret any inconvenience caused if addresses have changed or sites have ceased to exist, but can accept no responsibility for any such changes.

A catalogue record for this book is available from the British Library.

A catalog record for this book is available from the Library of Congress.

ISBN: HB: 978-1-3994-3022-7
       ePDF: 978-1-3994-3023-4
       ePub: 978-1-3994-3021-0

Typeset by RefineCatch Limited, Bungay, Suffolk
Printed and bound in Great Britain

For product safety related questions contact productsafety@bloomsbury.com.

To find out more about our authors and books visit www.bloomsbury.com
and sign up for our newsletters.

For all the colleagues who introduced me to the start-up world, taught and guided me along the way, my gratitude. Especially Stephan Dolezalek, Alan Salzman and Jim Marver of Vantage Point, Gijs Voskamp of Ludgate, and Nick Lyth of Green Angel.

CONTENTS

Acknowledgements xi
Preface xiii

1   The Horrible Premise of a Business Based on Failure 1

2   The World of Start-Ups and Their Backers 9
    The Venture Capitalist Mindset 9
    The Start-Up World: Through the Funding Lens 16
    The Causes of Failure 19

3   The First Cause of Failure: The Technology Doesn't Work 25
    The Whole Thing is a Fraud 26
    Flawed Premise 29
    Scale-Up Risk: Part 1 31
    Scale-Up Risk: Part 2 33
    Scale-Up Risk: Part 3 34
    The Technology Works (and It's Too Easy) 35
    What Does 'Work' Mean? 36
    Avoiding the Traps of the Technology That Doesn't Work 37
    Remember This to Improve Your Chance of Success 42

4   The Second Cause of Failure: The Market 45
    You've Got to Be Taught 46
    Too Many Customers 48
    Knowing the Route to Market 50
    Blame the Government 51
    A Great Opportunity – And Everyone Knows It 53
    The Problem of Getting Others to Stand Still 57

What We Learn to Do and Not to Do to Deal with the Market 58
Remember This to Improve Your Chance of Success 63

5 The Third Cause of Failure: Missing Engineers 65

Engineering: That's the Name of the Game 67
A Range of Problems 69
A Range of Engineering Disciplines 71
Engineering Quality 73
Get Someone Else to Do It for You 75
Getting Quantity and Quality of Engineers Right First Time 77
Remember This to Improve Your Chance of Success 82

6 The Fourth Cause of Failure: Leadership 83

Founders as Chief Executives: A Typology of Bad 84
Lead Me Not into Temptation 89
'Lifestyle' Companies 90
Are You Committed? 92
Companies Grow – Do Their Leaders? 93
Leadership Brought in from Outside 96
An Alternative Role for the Founder 97
Who Needs a Chief Financial Officer? 98
Leadership: What Type are You? How to Learn and Grow 100
Remember This to Improve Your Chance of Success 106

7 The Fifth Cause of Failure: The Board 107

The Company Leadership and the Board 108
What's the Rush on Governance? 110
How Boards Fail on Risk 111
Independent Directors 115
Investor Directors: The First Problem 117
Investor Directors: The Second Problem 119
Greed and Self-Deception 121
The Mentoring Role 122
Too Slow to Make a Change 123

Eliminating the Board as a Cause of Failure: Making it the Enabler of Success 125

Remember This to Improve Your Chance of Success 130

8 The Sixth Cause of Failure: Money or the Lack of It 131

Fundraising: The Different Stages Revisited 132
Analytic or Self-Deceiving 133
The Trap of Raising Too Little 134
Shortage of Cash Leads to False Economies 135
Failure through Constant Fundraising 137
Valuation: Neither Art Nor Science? 139
Money from the Government: Non-dilutive Funding or Distraction from Goal? 141
Money from the Government: Industrial Policy as a Trap 144
Working Capital: Not Knowing What You Don't Know 145
Later Stage Investment Failure Modes 147
It's Not Always about Money, but Often It is. Get This Right 149
Remember This to Improve Your Chance of Success 153

9 This, That, and the Other Thing 155

Focus, Pivot, or Quit 155
International Expansion 157
Founder Relationships 158
Marketing, Not Just Sales 159
More Involved, More Delegating? 161
Boring is Bad, or Good 162
Intellectual Property 163
Avoiding the Little Traps That Bite Your Ankle 166

10 We Can Do This Better 169

Finding a Successful Path 169
The Right Path: Making Investment Decisions More Efficient 172
The Right Path: Making Investment Decisions More Effective 174
Strategy and the Path to Success 177

People Making Decisions: Behavioural Economics for Start-Ups 193
People and Structure 200
A Path to Success 204

11 Could This Actually Work? 207

Index 211

ACKNOWLEDGEMENTS

Alex Davies, my editor at Bloomsbury, believed in this book from the first time I talked to her about it, and pushed me to articulate the positive steps that companies need to take to avoid failure, rather than just talk about the myriad ways to fail. As a result, this is a much better book.

I have always benefitted from friends who read my drafts and offer suggestions. I am particularly grateful to Simon Acland and Leah Lawrence for taking the time to make numerous comments on this manuscript, many of which have been incorporated.

And, of course, thanks to all the colleagues I had at Vantage Point – Stephan Dolezalek, Bill Green, David Fries; at Ludgate – Gijs and Jeroen Voskamp, Bill Weil, Nigel Meir; and at Green Angel – Simon Acland, Nick Lyth, Cam Ross; and many others at all three firms from whom I learned everything I know about venture investing. Likewise, the CEOs I have worked with and fellow board members, I am grateful to you all for putting up with my questions, challenges and occasional impatience.

PREFACE

Building a company is insanely hard. The number of things that you have to know. The amazing people that you have to surround yourself with. The adversaries and all the smart things that they're going to do. The adversities that you're going to be confronted with over time.
JENSEN HUANG[1]

Back in 2000, venture-capital funds raised $100 billion and put it into Internet start-ups – $100 billion! They would have been better off taking at least $50 billion of it, putting it into bushel baskets and lighting it on fire with an acetylene torch. That's the kind of madness you get with fee-driven investment management.
CHARLIE MUNGER[2]

Most new companies, start-ups, fail. An oft-repeated statistic places the fatality rate within one year at about 70 per cent. And that's true whether you are the clever person starting a new Thai/Italian fusion restaurant, or what you are sure will be the next Google, TikTok, Tesla, Novo Nordisk, whatever. Of the ones that don't fail quickly, many fail in years two, three, four, while others linger for a while, never quite able to provide a return on the money that was invested in them but never going out of business either. When investors do not get more money back than they could have received by simply investing in a fund tracking an index like the S&P 500, that is defined as a failure. As a founder, not only have you not become wealthy as a result of starting the company, but failing also means you have not been rewarded for what was certainly an extraordinary amount of work. Just as the investors could have done something else with the money, the founders could have spent their time working for a large company, or at a university, in a job that was reasonably secure and well paid. For a start-up to be a success from the founder perspective, they must make much more money than they could have made if they had taken the low-risk alternative career path. Or they must take away from the failure learnings that will serve them well in the thing they do next. It may be hard to put a value on such learning; in the right hands/mind it is worth a lot.

Most gurus of the start-up world say this high level of failure is inevitable. They often express the belief that the more you try to do something that is truly disruptive – whether in tech or healthcare or agriculture or fusion restaurants – a higher percentage of failure is to be expected. They assert that investing in a start-up is like placing a bet with a low probability of paying off, but if you make more bets, you will have a higher probability of coming out ahead in the end. Every compulsive bettor on horse racing knows that you cannot possibly come out ahead by betting on every horse in the race, and probably you cannot come out ahead by betting on the five with the best odds. Still, this is what the gurus of some start-up investment firms have convinced themselves is the sure way to make a fortune. To me, this thinking can be read as, 'We don't know what we're doing, although we put an awful lot of effort into making it look like we do, but if we do a lot, it will all be okay in the end.' It somehow feels pretty unsatisfactory.

I have always believed that in business we must learn. If something works spectacularly well, we should attempt to understand what we did to have that success. If we try something and it fails, what lessons do we learn, and how do we apply them next time? Learning of this sort is not superficial, though when it is done thoughtlessly it often turns out to be. I have sat in rooms with venture capital investors who, having heard a presentation from a biofuels company (for example), said, 'No, we invested in a biofuels company three years ago and it failed, so we shouldn't do that again.' This is not learning; it is extrapolation based on one data point. Learning would be saying, 'The previous biofuels firm we invested in had a perfectly good process. Our problem was that we didn't realize how much chemical engineering was required to go from lab to full-scale plant, so we didn't put the right resources in place. If we are going to back this company, that is one thing we need to do differently'.

This book is for founders *and* investors. It is for students and teachers of entrepreneurship, board members of early-stage companies, and perhaps most importantly for those who are thinking of how to turn their idea into a company, or started one last year and are struggling to understand why things might be going wrong. In it I am trying to examine the reasons failure occurs, recognizing that there are quite a few of them. If we can agree that these reasons are valid causes of failure, then we can learn when it is possible to avoid them. If we do that, then sometimes, maybe significantly more often than now, we prevent failures and turn them into moderate successes. That is the productive cycle of learning. If a failure is a company that fails to return to its owners more than the S&P 500 index, in the context of the technology start-up world, a moderate success is a company that, in a few years, returns two or three times (2x or 3x) the money invested to the investors and a similar return to the founders. By having a lot more of these moderate successes, rather than all of them being failures, we increase the chance of having one or two really spectacular (>100x) outcomes.

To understand why start-ups fail, a good place to start is with the structure and incentives of the venture capital industry, who are putting in most of the money that will underwrite these new, potentially disruptive, businesses. I will look at what I believe are the six main causes of failure, as well as some smaller ones, in each case trying to learn how to avoid these, or, if you are falling into a trap, how to get out of it successfully. The crucial thing about these causes is that most of them are avoidable if you have the awareness and the resources. Many of the highly successful disruptive businesses that are familiar names today faced down one or more of these potential causes of failure. After that, I am relentlessly positive and look at how start-ups get on a successful path and stay on it to grow an idea into a business.

Notes

1. "NVIDIA CEO Jensen Huang", *Acquired* (2023): https://www.acquired.fm/episodes/jensen-huang
2. "A Fireside Chat with Charlie Munger", Jason Zweig. *The Wall Street Journal* (2014): https://www.wsj.com/articles/BL-MBB-26843

1

The Horrible Premise of a Business Based on Failure

When I decided to retire from the very large oil company where I had spent eighteen years in executive roles, both technology and business, I spent quite a lot of time thinking about what I wanted to do next. After all, I was only sixty-one years old and didn't play golf, so there seemed no reason to actually retire. Now this was 2003, and there was a lot of talk and hype about venture capital, how it built businesses, drove innovation in products and made decisions faster and better than big corporations. I knew that my business life had been mainly about maintaining, improving and growing a big established business rather than starting something new. In that environment, technology innovation is not about disrupting. It is usually about squeezing a fraction of a penny of improvement out of an existing process because the throughput is so great. As for product innovation, while people were talking about how innovative technology businesses came out with new products every six months, the oil industry had only had two major new products since the Second World War, and one of those was the result of legislation! I wanted to experience this different world of venture capital for myself, for three reasons:

> I always felt that in your working life you should be both doing and studying what others were doing. When I was a young professor I studied

how senior faculty ran their research groups; as a university department Chair and later as a dean, I observed the good and bad behaviours of the deans, provosts and presidents with whom I worked, as well as learned from industry executives on our board or in advisory roles. Later, as an executive in industry, I saw how other senior executives did things that were very effective and tried to put them into my own voice. I also saw bad behaviour, most commonly bullying, and learned how not to do that. I wanted to learn how venture capitalists, this new-ish tribe, did business.

In the early part of this century, it had become clear that the world of energy was changing. I had been involved in measures to mitigate climate change for several years, especially ways of thinking about
how to stabilize and reverse its effects. By 2003, many people believed climate change to be the critical issue that would shape the new century. It seemed that the venture capital world could be at least a part of this massive change – seeding, nurturing, growing and ultimately disrupting the existing energy infrastructure. I understood a lot about energy and had something to bring to the venture world, if I could find a firm that wanted to commit to it.

The third reason was that venture capitalists seemed to make outsized rewards for their work. I had been well rewarded by my employers but did not have the big upside potential that a successful partner in a venture firm seemed to have. I wanted to do it to make more money.

Perhaps I should have made a systematic study of the leading firms, talked to several, seen who was interested in me and who I liked. Life, at least my working life, has never seemed to evolve in that way. About two months before my last working day in 2003, I was approached by two venture guys from California, from Vantage Point Venture Partners, a mid-sized firm, who had experienced considerable success with hardware, software and healthcare ventures, and wanted to get into what they now called Cleantech. Over the course of several conversations in London and California I met the leaders of the firm, helped them think about other people they might bring in, and together we evolved a strategy for raising a new fund to make some investments. Over the next decade I got to help as we raised money, chose companies to back, rejected many investments, co-invested with other venture firms (in both California and Boston, the two big centres for this in the US, and with some international venture firms) and corporate partners, served on boards of several different start-up companies, had a few successes and a lot of failures.

Towards the end of my time with the Californians, I began to work with Ludgate Investments, a London-based venture firm, and saw the world of start-ups from a different point of view, because while there are commonalities of practice there are also hugely dissimilar cultures around venture investing in different geographies. Culture aside, there was one striking thing that was common to both: there were a few successes and a lot of failures.

And then in 2018 I was introduced to the world of angel investing, backing the early stage of companies, through what was then known as Green Angel Syndicate, later Green Angel Ventures. Here it is not a venture capital firm making decisions on whether to invest, rather individual investors (angels) coming together, listening, evaluating (with some helpers) and deciding to back a company, or not. More decisions, more boards, and – well, too soon to say whether any big successes; certainly a number of our investments headed for failure.

All of this has been and continues to be a lot of fun, certainly a chance to work with wonderful colleagues, combined with a chance to observe, study and learn. One question intrigued me from among the many things I learned: What are the causes of such a high percentage of failures of start-up companies? If we can agree on these failure modes, then are there steps, actions or behaviours that can be taken to avoid them happening?

What we love to read and hear about, in articles, books, newsletters and podcasts, are the spectacular successes in this venture capital world – the likes of Amazon, Apple, Facebook/Meta, Tesla, Genentech, and others ... Occasionally we get to read about the spectacular failures, like Better Place,[1] founded in 2007, which raised $850 million in series A and B funding rounds, and declared itself bankrupt in 2013, its assets and intellectual property (IP) being sold for $450,000. My California colleagues and I were among the most enthusiastic Better Place investors. Or even more spectacular, Jawbone,[2] whose valuation rose to close to $4 billion just before it went bankrupt. What we don't read about are the unspectacular failures. There are thousands of them. Companies that wound up, after months or years, being worth approximately nothing. And another vast group of venture capital funded companies that, while promising to be worth 10x or 100x what was invested in them, end up being worth between 0.5x and 1x, which is also failure using my definition.

The technology start-up world is *not* the world of numerous spectacular successes – it is the world of a few great successes and many failures. An analysis by Y Combinator, a backer of early-stage companies, showed that of 280 investments, 75 per cent of their payback came from two companies, with most of the rest contributing zero. This may exaggerate the problem, which is undoubtedly going to be worse for early-stage companies, but not by much. Even the best of the venture funds work on the belief that if they make 10x investments, one will be an enormous success, three to four will more or less break even and six to seven will fail. Peter Thiel, who is a legendary figure in Silicon Valley, says that in any big venture fund, the top company will equal or outperform the entire rest of the fund.[3] This is not a good starting proposition for a venture capital business: miss that one immense success and the whole fund is a flop.

Increasingly, over the past two decades, I have wondered if the remarkably high percentage of failures is really required in this universe of disruptive innovation, or whether it is possible to do better. This book is an examination of what causes all of these failures, trying to dig into the details of failure as I have seen it happen, and then to ask, 'Ok, we see that trap, how do we avoid it?' This then leads to, 'How can this all have a substantially better outcome for my company, or across a large number of companies in which I am investing?' It is a personal view, based on my observations, learnings, and experience – not a systematic academic study of failure, which would use case histories, look at a large representative sample and from these derive a model of how to improve.

Entrepreneurs are not cautious by nature. They believe they see a gap in the market, an unsolved problem, and have a way to fill that gap, so they plunge in. The greatest entrepreneurial inventors, like Thomas Edison, did this over and over again. Some of the greats did it once, like Charles Martin Hall who discovered a way to make aluminium from its ore at what became a 97 per cent reduction in cost from existing processes, founding the Pittsburgh Reduction Company, which eventually became Alcoa. Maybe these inventors saw the risks, maybe they just dove in. Even if they did see the dangers, they had tremendous self-belief in their ability to overcome them. In this book, I am trying to help entrepreneurs see what hazards lie under the water before they take the plunge, so there is a chance they won't crash right into them.

Investors are by nature a more cautious but still adventurous lot. They have worked hard to get someone to trust them with a lot of money, or have earned a lot of money themselves, and would prefer not to just make an obvious mistake and lose it, which would markedly reduce their ability to raise money again. Still, they believe in themselves, just as the entrepreneurs do. They like the spirit of adventure that comes with investing in the next big thing that others haven't spotted. In the culture that exists for the investors, however, the dominant mode of thinking is, 'A lot of what we are investing in is going to fail. It is necessary that we have a lot of failures if we are to have one or two big wins. Besides, there is no point in dwelling on why failures occur, because we are adventurous.'

Now a challenge that some will raise to a book about the causes of failure in start-ups is that it will make both the entrepreneur and the investor overly cautious. Read this book, they will say, and you will never start any companies or make any investments because all you will see is how the company can fail, rather than how it can succeed. They will say that there are a lot of unknowns (and to quote Donald Rumsfeld, at least some of these are likely to be unknown unknowns) in what leads to the great successes, and you must trust that these are going to actually happen.

Well, I don't agree. We are not casino gamblers at the roulette wheel, expecting a large number of failures and the occasional big win. We are business people. In almost any other business enterprise, the number of complete failures and very low return investments that we have come to accept in founding and investing in start-ups would be unacceptable. An exception might be making and releasing new movies, which certainly involves a lot of upfront investment of time and money, yet with only about 35–40 per cent making a profit. **Business is about taking risk, and you only make money by taking risks, but we do it with eyes wide open, most importantly with thoughtful processes that take risk off the table whenever we can.**

What do we mean by risk in this context? It is not the risk that you will mortgage your house to fund the start-up and lose everything, or that you will take money from a venture capital fund and lose all of that. Sure, those things can happen; they are not risks, they are outcomes. By risk I mean that as we start to build a product, try to sell it, grow the business, and respond to competitors effectively, there are numerous unknown or unanticipated things that could happen. These risks, which are all around us, can sink the business, unless we find ways to manage them. This book is a guide to where those risks exist for start-ups, because only when you know where the risks are is it possible for them to be mitigated. I am trying to provide a guide to intelligent start-up risk identification for both entrepreneurs and investors. Having identified each major risk, I offer up a bunch of suggestions about how to deal with those risks.

Even risk mitigation is not enough. A company needs to get on a successful path from the start and find ways to continue on that path. After examining what I believe are the main causes of failure, and considering how to deal with them effectively, I turn this discussion around at the end of the book and talk about how to get – and stay – on a path with a higher probability of success.

Notes

1   'Better Place (company)', Wikipedia, https://en.wikipedia.org/wiki/Better_Place_(company), accessed 24 June 2025.

2   'Jawbone: The Rise and Fall of the First Wearable Technology Company | Sequoia Capital', https://www.sequoiacap.com/podcast/crucible-moments-jawbone/, accessed 24 June 2025. Sequoia is to be commended for trying to learn the lessons from this spectacular failure, an all-too-rare occurrence in the venture capital world.

3   Peter Thiel with Blake Masters, *Zero to One* (New York, NY: Crown Business, 2014).

2

The World of Start-Ups and Their Backers

All companies were once start-ups.[1]

The Venture Capitalist Mindset

To leave whatever you were doing, or the career path you were on, and start a company based on an idea, is a big risk. To invest in such a start-up company rather than in the S&P 500 tracker fund, you must have the self-belief that enables you to take that big risk. There are lots of great ideas, and very few of them lead to great companies, or even to great returns for the investors who backed them at an early stage in their life. When the venture involves technology (not all of them do – there are venture funds that invest in shoe or clothing companies, or in businesses that provide health care) you add all the risks of any new business venture and overlay the ability to make the technology work successfully.

I am going to describe how venture capital funds work. If you are an entrepreneur reading this, you might think, 'I don't really care about that, once I have their money I am going to do my thing.' Well, turns out that once they give you that first tranche of money, they have attached a whole bunch of strings to you and your business that can either help it succeed or cause it to fail. You need to understand what is motivating the people who have given you money. It is naive to just say, 'Well, they gave me money to make me successful, believing that their investment will return many times what they put in.' Their structure, how and when they are rewarded, is more complicated than that. As an entrepreneur you need to understand it, because incentives drive behaviours.

Most of the money for venture capital funds does not come from the individuals making decisions on the investments. (This is completely different with angel investors, a group I will discuss further, who usually make individual decisions on whether to invest.) It may come from wealthy families who have entrusted a small portion of their wealth to a venture capital partnership, either directly or through an intermediary, or from a pension fund that allocates a small share of its participants' money to higher risk investments. Sometimes it comes from a corporation that wants to dip its toe into a new area. These investors, in the most common structure, are Limited Partners (LPs) in the venture fund, and the people making the decisions on how to invest the money, the Venture Fund as an entity, is the General Partner (GP).

The mindset that develops among GPs is a direct result of their reward structure with respect to the LPs. The GP takes a small amount of the money they are given to pay salaries and expenses, usually no more than 2 per cent annually. The salaries are good but not more than an executive in a large firm would earn, probably less. Moreover, partners in the venture firm are generally required to put a modest amount of their personal money into the fund. As investments mature and are sold or go through an initial public offering (IPO), the first obligation of the GP is to pay back the investment of the LPs.[2] After that, the GP has what is called a carried interest in the fund and gets 20 per cent (usually) of additional returns. The goal of the GP is to get past this threshold with the LPs, because then they make some real money.

Supposing you invest in a start-up as an individual and the result is that an investment of $1 million, on sale or IPO three years later, is worth $1.5 million.

If you are an individual doing this you might think, fine, I did OK on that. In fact, using my previous definition of 'not failure', outperforming the S&P 500, OK would be the answer, because in recent years that has had a three-year return of about 33 per cent, and over the longer term that was 23–24 per cent. However, if you are the GP, and you realize that many of the companies will fail because they are risky, then you think, I'll never get to my carried interest with that kind of definition of success.

Let's do an oversimplified calculation. If the GP raised a fund of $10 million and ran it for five years, they have $9 million available to invest after expenses. Suppose they made nine investments of $1 million each, and say, very optimistically, seven of them returned $1.5 million as in our earlier example, and two failed, then the net takings are $10.5 million. Now you pay back the LPs their $9 million after the 2 per cent for expenses, plus 80 per cent of the remaining $1.5 million, and you are left with a paltry $300,000 as a reward over and above your salary for all your effort. This just doesn't work.

To be financially successful in this model the approach has to be as follows: If I make nine investments of $1 million each, one of them has to be worth $100 million when I exit, then maybe three or four break even or make a small profit, and the other five probably fail, but I don't care. Now you've invested $9 million, have yielded $103 million, paid the LPs back their $9 million plus 80 per cent of the remaining $94 million, and you have $18.8 million to share among the employees (the leadership of whom are partners) in the GP, remembering that these employees/partners have already been paid salaries for their work. It turns out that in the US, and some other countries, this $18.8 million is not subject to normal income tax, rather it is treated as capital gains, meaning it is worth a lot more. In any case, you don't care very much about the five complete duds and the three others that didn't deliver what they promised. The one big winner in the second case has led to a result that is 63,000 per cent better for the venture firm, even though the number of complete failures is larger.

In this example, I have not considered the variable of time. It's pretty obvious that getting a multiple of your money back in three years is a different result from getting it back in six or ten years. In business we have a standard way of figuring this out, effectively applying a discount to the money you get back in later years. This discount should relate to either what it would cost you to borrow the money you invested, or what you might earn from the money you have invested if you put it into a safe investment instead. By using this standard method, we can calculate what is called the Internal (sometimes Investors) Rate of Return (IRR). When venture groups decide to make an investment, they will usually make a bunch of assumptions about how long it will take for the company to achieve a certain value, exiting from their investment via either a sale of the company or floating it as a public company (an Initial Public Offering or IPO), and then calculate the IRR they expect. You can be sure that every one of their investments using this method and these assumptions led to a large positive IRR being calculated, even if in practice they have rarely achieved their assumptions. The IRRs of the individual investments roll up into an IRR of the venture capital fund. Investors in the fund will use this as a measure of whether to give the venture capital firm more money the next time they come begging.

Now it is this arithmetic that shapes investment decisions and becomes deeply imbued in the mindset of all those sitting in the room deciding whether to back your company or reject it. While you are pitching your idea, the venture capital partners are thinking, 'If these guys succeed with the impossible dream they are proposing, will it be a big win?' 'Because if they fail,' the thinking goes, 'all I can lose is the money I invested, but if they succeed, however unlikely that may be, the sky's the limit!' It is this seemingly uncapped upside outcome that differentiates venture investing from betting on all the horses in a race or all the numbers on the roulette table.

That's the key step in the mental model. If you believe that it is possible you will get one of the big winners – the next Facebook, Netflix, Tesla – then you pick companies that have the most potential for disruption and back them. In baseball metaphor, which is often used in Silicon Valley venture speak, you certainly aren't trying to hit singles, you don't just go for home runs, but for grand slams.[3] And, as is well known in baseball, if you try to hit a lot of home runs you will strike out a lot. Bringing things back to venture investing, the prevailing dogma is that we should expect to have a lot of failures, because this is a consequence of our very investment strategy. Failure is inevitable. We don't worry that there are a lot of failures, because we will get a few big wins. Sebastian Mallaby wrote a whole book saying that it is a *law* that at best 20 per cent of the investments will generate 80 per cent of the returns.[4]

As a venture capitalist, I heard this over and over in the room where companies were presenting to us (pitching their company, the slides they used known as the pitch deck), and decisions were being made on investing the funds we had raised. True, there was a lot of rational analysis of the companies we considered, the ones we funded and the ones we rejected. There was subsequently an enormous amount of hard work done by the partners in our firm on the companies we chose to invest in, as they struggled through their journey attempting to become big, successful businesses. Note that all this hard work, which is a cost over and above the money invested, is another thing that differentiates venture investing from gambling.

Here is a conundrum: Success in this model is predicated on getting a few very big wins. The model says it is inevitable that a lot of companies in which you invest will fail. Of course, investors do not know at the outset which is the one that will be the big win, and usually we still don't know two or three years later, meaning we put in a huge amount of effort (and often we continue to inject funds) on all or most of them. We use our experience and intelligence to select companies that we believe will be highly successful, after which we do what we believe is our best effort to make them successful, or at least to keep them from failing. Still, we expect most of them to fail.

It is not just the partners and junior staff in the venture firm putting in this effort – making contacts, sitting through difficult board meetings, navigating crises when cash is short or a key employee leaves. Certainly, more than 95 per cent of the effort is by the entrepreneurs and the staff of the company that has received the investment. We all know that they are working long hours, under stress, not taking vacations, to make their company a success. Yet there is an expectation that they will fail. Why has no one laid out what are the causes of failure, and how to avoid them? **Failure should not be an expectation. It is a bad result that can sometimes be avoided.**

In this book I am going to examine the thinking and the actions that can help us find a way out of this conundrum. I will ask whether there are things that we could anticipate that would have dissuaded us from investing in something doomed to fail – things that we, as entrepreneurs and investors, could do at the outset of the investment to make a company successful rather than a failure, and, for most of the book, things that we could do differently in the life of the company that would have made a difference. In other words, I am going to examine the causes of failure from before the first injection of funding through the development of the business, and in each case I am going to suggest how not to fall victim to them.

I assert that the causes of failure I am going to examine, and the ways to avoid these causes, can help a venture capital group achieve meaningful positive returns (say on the order of 3x the money invested) from a significantly larger number of companies. Avoiding these failures, getting these good positive returns, will not in itself lead to more companies that return 100x their investment. The huge returns come both from a rare business success and from the financial markets (whether through IPO or acquisition) with a strong dose of what Alan Greenspan once called in another context 'irrational exuberance'.

When the conditions are there to produce a big winner, there is sometimes more than one competitor. An exception to this is usually with pharmaceuticals, though even in the 2020 race for Covid vaccines there were many companies with teams attempting to produce one quickly, and several of them did not produce a viable product. There were numerous search engines, yet Google is omnipresent. Some of the causes of failure that are discussed in this book are what make the difference between the winners and also-rans in these areas. Leadership of the company, of course. Board actions or inactions, and the interplay between the entrepreneurial leadership and the board. Engineering the product so that it can be manufactured at a competitive cost and work at extraordinary levels of reliability. How the company digs in to understand the market, where necessary educating the target customer segment to want the product it is offering. Money, where it comes from, is it sufficient, how it affects decision-making. These things can make the difference between becoming what Professor James Utterback called the 'dominant design',[5] the one that wins out in a competitive field, and the companies with good, even the best, technology that still disappear.

The outcome of fewer failures with a larger number of modest successes is well worth going for. If we can convert even half of the 70–80 per cent failures into 3x successes, that starts to look like a meaningfully better performance of the fund. With more 3x successes there is a greater chance of a 100x outcome, and certainly a higher probability of some 5–10x companies. Perhaps more important, it leads to a whole bunch of viable, thriving businesses that underpin a growth economy. While every entrepreneur reading this book wants to be the 100x success, they would much rather be the 3x company than a failure. To achieve this, entrepreneurs need to know how to deal with the traps waiting to kill their company.

Companies that fail early because of **avoidable** causes can never achieve even moderate success, let alone 100x success. Some books and articles on start-ups urge entrepreneurs to fail quickly. In most cases this advice is just silly because it ignores the truth that to build a business takes time. Still, early failure is occasionally preferable, as it avoids several follow-on investments that have no return. It saves you spending several more years of your life on an idea that is not going to work. We need to be able to distinguish between a business idea that is flawed, needing to be shut down quickly, and a sound idea that just takes time to be built into a viable enterprise. In addition to personal satisfaction, it is certainly a lot more rewarding for both the leaders/employees of the start-up and the investors to have a modest success than a failure. For all these reasons it is worth exploring why start-ups fail.

The Start-Up World: Through the Funding Lens

Not all start-ups need to take money from venture capitalists; most of them don't because they are small businesses designed to remain small. The new dry cleaners, hardware store or dental surgery has a predictable set of economics and can usually get the financing it needs from a bank. I will have more to say about debt financing when we talk about sources of money. Occasionally, start-ups achieve a certain amount of market traction early, get some meaningful revenues that can fuel expansion, and don't need to take other people's money to grow and succeed. There are a few notable examples of giant, successful companies that bootstrapped their way up from nothing to large scale. Other than some pure software companies, perhaps the most notable example is Ikea, which never took any external investment or debt.

These are exceptions. When you are starting a business that is an adventure into the unknown, building the product that the world did not know it needs, solving the problem that some thought couldn't be solved, or disrupting the established player that seems like it cannot be dislodged from its dominant position, you need money from people who are willing to take a bigger risk than a bank. That is the world of what is broadly defined as venture capital.

In fact, it is several worlds, interlinked and related, but distinct, usually by stage. It's worth defining these stages, because a company is born, like a baby, very small and with not too much of an idea of what it is going to be when it grows up. Unlike a baby, from the start it must make numerous choices – however, it is always in danger of dying before it realizes its potential or the potential that others see in it. At least in part this is about money, the food for development and growth that is the start-up equivalent of breast milk. What follows is an elementary guide to this, laden with some of my prejudices.

The first stage is a little bit of money to try something and show that you have an idea worth taking forward. Generally, it is called 'seed funding'. Maybe it comes from friends and family, or by mortgaging the founder's house (a form of bank debt where the founder is taking most of the risk, rather than the bank). Sometimes governments or universities have funds to get companies started from nothing more than an idea or a few lab experiments. If a government will give you this money without taking an ownership stake in the company, just because it wants to encourage entrepreneurship or the development of a particular industry, of course you should grab it.

Then you might attract some individuals, of varying degrees of sophistication, with money they can afford to lose, who think they can spot a winner, and these are called angel investors. While there are individual angels who usually have a particular interest in which they invest, these days angel investors often work together, perhaps employing someone to screen companies that they should consider for investment, sit as a group to listen to these companies pitch, hear each other's questions, then make an individual decision about whether to invest. A twenty-first-century innovation at this early stage is crowdfunding, where you might get hundreds of (sometimes gullible) individuals to each put in a small amount of money, thinking that it is an easy way for them to get rich. Usually, they make this decision based on a description or a short video about the company. Crowdfunding investors tend to have unrealistic ideas about how much influence they can have over the company for the small amount of money they have invested. This can lead to them being a pain for the company leadership to deal with. However, if you have a retail product that relies on individuals deciding to adopt it, a few thousand enthusiastic investors from crowdfunding might be worth the pain because they can be useful in spreading the word.

Next comes early-stage venture capital, which may still be from high net worth individuals or angel investors. More often it is in larger amounts from the venture capital firms with the GP/LP structure I have described, in what is called the A round. There are some firms that particularly target this first round of funding. Then as things are derisked, or appear to be, later stage, B, C and so on rounds may happen. As you go through these rounds of funding, the company, at least on paper, is seen as more valuable. Each stage has attached to it a 'valuation' or a 'pre-money valuation' – what the entrepreneurs think it's worth before new money has been invested. This determines what the investor's cheque buys in terms of a share of the company, while for the entrepreneur it is what percentage of your ownership you are giving up in exchange for the money. I will have more to say about valuation later, because it sometimes becomes part of the cause for failure. While new investors often enter the company's shareholder roll in later rounds, many A round investors will reserve money to 'follow on' in B and C, sometimes enough to preserve their percentage shareholding if their fund is large enough. By contrast, the very early-stage investors generally will not be able to accomplish this; they just hope that the pie is getting really big so that eventually their early bet will pay off. Assuming they do follow on, the fund of the A round investor becomes progressively more and more committed to the company. The size of its bet, in terms of percentage of the fund, has increased, and the penalty for failure, in terms of fund results, becomes greater. On the other hand, it has acquired some of its shares at a low valuation. On a good exit these can be returning far more to their fund than the funds of those who bought shares at a higher price.

It is important to point out that not all shares in a company are necessarily equal. They might have different rights in terms of voting on key decisions the company has to make, such as whether to take in new investment or whether to sell the company. Often investors ask for certain preferred positions for their shares – that is, when the company is sold, they get their money back first. These sorts of preference rights can materially affect the reward that founders receive.

Corporations, as already mentioned, occasionally put money into a venture capital fund. More common is that many corporations, and not just the very largest ones, have their own internal venture arm, investing in early-stage companies that have technology that might be of interest to them. This corporate venture capital often comes in at A round stage, sometimes on its own, more often alongside a venture fund. I will have more to say about the good, the bad, and the ugly of this in my discussion of the role of the board.

One more point relating to the ownership of founders and other employees. It is quite common that in any of the funding rounds from A onwards a pool of shares is created for the employees, which may or may not include the founders (who already own a significant stake). A figure like 10 per cent of the total shares is often used. These are not distributed at once, at least some of them being reserved for key employees not yet hired. They are usually awarded as options linked to certain achievements, specifically to increased valuation of the company. Depending on the numbers and structure of the share options, taking venture capital into the company does not necessarily lead to the founders' share being reduced proportionately, assuming they achieve their goals.

The Causes of Failure

What I have just described through the funding lens is one way of looking at the typology of the start-up world. It is a process of invention or innovation, which starts out as all risk with low valuation, and is (hopefully) progressively derisked until it becomes a normal business, maybe a valuable public company trading on a stock exchange. Perhaps it is acquired by a big company to become part of its product offering, or remains a private company controlled by its founders, such as Ikea or at a much smaller but still significant scale, MathWorks. This process of growth is usually about scale-up – going from making one or two of some sort of widget, to hundreds, thousands, millions. It can also be about solving the problem of going from a chemical process making grams of product in a lab or pilot plant to making tonnes of product in a first plant. Or it can be a software product with a few features used by a limited set of customers, to one with more bells and whistles used by millions. Although I won't spend much time on start-ups that only offer advisory or consulting services in this book, they are an important class of companies that frequently manage to build themselves to scale without taking capital from venture firms, in part because they don't need it, but largely because most venture firms find such companies completely uninteresting.

Scale-up has all kinds of challenges, and failure to meet these challenges leads to many of the failures. Each stage requires more capital, and in countries where there is a vibrant start-up culture there is an infrastructure to provide that capital for every stage. How much capital is needed will vary greatly by the sort of product or innovation that the company is setting out to make. Some software innovations require smaller amounts of capital to demonstrate their capability, with funds mainly needed for engineers/developers and marketing. By contrast, a company that wants to displace a major chemical or fuel product may require a billion dollars just to design, build, and operate its first full-scale plant. Some of the causes of failure I am going to examine in this book are more prevalent in the latter group; however, most of them apply to both groups.

A look at the literature about the venture capital world, particularly the Silicon Valley world, reveals little about the causes of failure. Where writers do speak about it, they attribute failures to bad luck or bad timing. Of course, this is ridiculous. There may be a luck or a timing element to the outrageous successes, based around coming to market when sentiment leads to higher than rational valuations for certain technological areas. Yet the people involved, both entrepreneurs and investors, in these successes never say it was luck. It was always because of their ability to see a gap in the market, the brilliant leadership they brought to the company, how they broke the rules or made new rules. Never because they were lucky. I would assert that luck has an extraordinarily small role to play in failure. There can be, and are, a few exceptions, for example a company is based around the brilliance of one person, and he or she is killed in a plane crash or a skiing accident. It has happened and might account for one or two of the tens of thousands of failures that have occurred. As to timing, sure, it is harder to have rapid growth in a period like 2008–9 when there was a severe economic downturn. That also accounts for an exceedingly small percentage of the failures in the last twenty-five years.

Occasionally in the literature of the overwhelming statistics on start-up failure there is an attempt at figuring out the causes, and the authors make a different mistake – they decide it must be one thing. There are articles that say, 'I have studied the failures of a large group of start-ups and it is overwhelmingly because they overestimated the size of the market,' or, 'I have studied start-up failures from a range of venture firms and it is always because co-founders fell out with each other.' If only life were that simple. There are many causes, and a start-up that is absolutely solid on one aspect may be very weak on another.

In the chapters that follow I will explore the main reasons for failure that have nothing to do with luck and little to do with timing. In looking at the failures, I'm going to distinguish between the following:

- This was never going to work, it should not have been funded. The founders either knew it wouldn't work or could have found out by getting a little advice.

- This could have worked if it had the right leadership, rather than the person who founded and wanted to lead it.

- This could have worked if we changed leadership when the company moved to the next stage.

- This worked at small scale and would have been a success (maybe someone else later made it a success) but the company didn't know how to convert small scale to large scale.

- It all worked, sadly we didn't understand the market, so nobody bought the product, or we didn't focus on the most promising product that the market wanted, preferring to keep inventing a lot of products.

- The technology worked, however the board screwed up a perfectly good company by its actions – or lack of actions – or by the board members pulling in different directions.

- Timidity – the company decided to grow slowly when there was a big opportunity, leading to the founders being repeatedly engaged in fundraising instead of growing the business.

From these distinctions come six main causes of failure that can serve as a guide to doing something, probably to doing everything, differently. After I discuss those six causes, there are a number of small (and not so small) things that cause failure that I will discuss briefly. Don't ignore these either!

As I have already made clear, this is a personal, not a statistical, analysis of thousands of failures, though I respect people who do such studies.[6] In my experience of working in venture capital, decisions about investments are made by people listening, analysing, agonizing, and then going with their gut feeling about the CEO or the extent of disruption, mostly by convincing themselves of the possibility for a big win. Likewise, in the exploration of the causes of failure and ways to overcome them that follows, I have done some analysing but I am mainly recounting my experiences failing with my own start-ups that wanted to build solar farms in Nigeria and Saudi Arabia, sitting as a venture capital partner on numerous company pitches, listening to the trials and tribulations of my partners with companies they are struggling to help succeed, and being in the boardroom (sometimes as Chair) of several start-up companies myself. Combined with reading and listening and learning. Always learning.

Notes

1 The epigraph is a paraphrasing of the well-known statement about art, 'All art was once contemporary.' Yes, even Standard Oil and General Electric were once start-ups.

2 Often they must pay this back plus some modest premium, known as the 'hurdle rate', but for simplicity I ignore this in these model calculations.

3 For those not of an American baseball persuasion, a grand slam is when a batter hits a home run and there are runners on all bases, resulting in four runs being scored. It is a flawed metaphor to say venture should go for grand slams, because in order to hit a grand slam, three other players must have hit singles. For those of a more cricket than baseball persuasion, it would be a batter who always tries for a six.

4 Sebastian Mallaby, *The Power Law* (London: Penguin 2022).

5 James M. Utterback, *Mastering the Dynamics of Innovation* (Cambridge, MA: Harvard University Press, 1994), 23.

6 The best book-length study of start-up failure I have found is by Tom Eisenmann at Harvard University, *The Fail Safe Start-Up* (London: Penguin, 2021). It is worth reading and is very different from this book.

3

The First Cause of Failure
The Technology Doesn't Work

When a company is seeking investment, it usually starts by saying, 'Well, here's a problem, here's the prize available to the person or firm that solves that problem, and here's my solution, the technology I am going to bring to the market.' Sometimes they are bolder, and say, 'Here's a problem people don't even know they have, there is a whole industry out there believing their future is secure, and I am going to completely disrupt it.' Now the venture capitalist sees the bold person standing in front of the room (pitching), or staring out from a screen, and says, 'Okay, this looks like a real entrepreneur.' Then they say, 'I can verify the size of the prize, and probably in a few phone calls decide whether the market is ready for it, or maybe could be made ready for it, so that leaves the tech. Does it actually work?' This is a different question from, 'I have seen you build one of them, can you build lots of them, and do it profitably?' We will come on to the question of going from lab or pilot scale to full-scale in terms of the company's ability to manufacture widgets or distribute software to millions of users when I consider why not having sufficient engineering capability leads to failure. For now, in addition to other questions about, 'Does the technology actually work?' I will discuss the possibility that there are several fatal scale-up risks present at the outset, meaning that the technology can never work at scale.

So right up front, before a first investment is made, should I believe what I am being told? This might seem like a yes or no question, but even so it could be challenging to answer. When we dig into it there are several aspects. Unless the potential investors have figured out that the technology works, using expertise and resources at their disposal, there is a danger that failure has been built into the investment from the start, and it can be an expensive failure too. This is not just the investors' problem. The founders stand up and make a convincing case that the technology works. Have they made a realistic assessment before they commit to spending the next several years on it? If it is a group of founders, one of whom is the 'inventor brain', have the others done their due diligence on the technology that they are staking a part of their careers and personal wealth on? This first cause of failure is different from the next five I am going to discuss. For those five, I will assert that failure is avoidable if you have the wisdom, experience and money to do the right thing. When the technology is inherently flawed, for reasons that we will discuss, that is not the case. The best outcome, certainly for investors and probably for the founders, is that the company does not receive any funding. Let's dig deeper into this first cause of failure: Does the technology actually work?

The Whole Thing is a Fraud

The case of Theranos, which promised blood tests using a drop of blood rather than the usual 30 ml, has been well publicized. The founder is in prison. Sadly, this is far from an isolated case. Other well-documented cases include Nikola, Headspin, Outcome Health, Lily Robotics, Paycoin, and uBiome. Every venture investor listening to a pitch needs to be alert to the possibility of fraud – and by the way, fraudsters can be excellent at delivering a convincing pitch.

Some years ago, a prominent member of the House of Lords in the UK approached a fellow member saying that he and two others were working with a young entrepreneur who had a revolutionary new way to make fuel from waste products. Let's call it Fastspin Company. 'Would you be interested in this?' they asked. 'Well,' he said, 'I would have to be convinced that it was real.' 'What would that take to convince you? Do you want to meet the entrepreneur?' 'No, but if you can get Bernie Bulkin to evaluate it and he is convinced then I will look at it.'

Thus it happened that one morning I met with Lord R, over coffee, and he explained this to me. I told him that while I didn't usually do any consulting of this sort, considering who had referred them to me I would do it on two conditions: that what you want is a genuine evaluation of the technology, not just a puff piece saying how great it is, and that you will pay me £3,500/day for my work. He assured me that both of those conditions were absolutely fine.

Lord R and I then met with two other backers of the company. None of them had any technical ability or background in the technology in question; still, they were all seasoned business people. Once again, I made clear the terms under which I was doing the evaluation. Then we met the entrepreneur, who seemed both enthusiastic and determined. He gave me pages of diagrams explaining the innovative reactor he had designed and how it worked, told me about a demonstration plant built and operated in Italy, gave me pages of data from the plant, and in answer to a question, said that he had filed several patents on the technology.

Everything about this turned out to be fraudulent. There was no plant in Italy and never had been. The design was not original. It was copied from some papers and patents published in Russian, which I found in about two minutes. He had not filed any patents but once had a visit with some patent lawyers. The data, when I analysed them, were easily seen to be made up, and not very skilfully either. It took me two days to figure this out, and another day to draft a report documenting it. My report didn't please the backers at all. They never paid me for my work, despite saving them from continuing to invest in a complete fraud.

Lily Robotics was a company that claimed to have a powerful new sort of drone;[1] however, it turned out that the video it showed investors was stock footage taken from the internet, and the prototype it had built was non-functional. uBiome simply falsified the test results that it gave its customers.[2] PayCoin was a Ponzi scheme where new money was used to pay off earlier investors.[3]

Over the course of several years, I saw other frauds of various sorts, most not so extensive as these, though having some of the same traits. In one case, I listened to a presentation where the data looked too good to be true, and when I questioned it, the presenters admitted it was a drawing rather than actual data from lab instruments. Still, they assured me that the data would look like that once they did the experiment.

Another kind of fraud is concealing from investors the lack of novelty of the technology. Fastspin Company was one version of this, where a cursory search turned up Russian publications doing the same thing. Another was a company presenting a novel desalination technology to angel investors. The pitch was, 'Here are the problems with the two main types of desalination in use today, and here is the radical innovative approach I have invented.' Well, as it happened, I knew about this approach, because my colleagues in California and I had considered investing in a UK company that did exactly the same thing, and a friend of mine in the US had been CEO of another company trying to use this technical approach as well. This entrepreneur pitching to us never mentioned either of them.

Most of the pitches I have heard over the last twenty years have not been frauds. There have been a small number, some slightly fraudulent (one or two false pieces of data), some more blatant. Investors must always be alert to fraud because the number is small but will guarantee that you lose all your money and some of your reputation. I also caution founder scientists and engineers never to yield to the temptation to present data or information that you know to be fraudulent. You are probably standing in front of a group of people, asking for their money, because you have some sort of reputation based on accomplishments. This is hard-won but easily destroyed by even small amounts of bad behaviour. Do not think of this as a game, because it is one that you will lose.

How to detect a fraud is the key question. The very partial list of frauds I gave at the beginning of this section shows that investors can be taken in. I think this is an argument for a very particular kind of diversity. When there is not a single person in the room with a degree in Chemistry, Physics, or Chemical Engineering, the chances that you will invest in something that violates the Second Law of Thermodynamics goes way up! If you have raised a fund to invest in novel biotechnology, better be sure there are a few people in the room who can understand the complexities of CRISPR. At the beginning of the California venture capital ecosystem in the late 1950s, all the leading investors were electrical engineers, and most of the companies they were looking at were electronics related. They could understand what they were being told and ask tough questions. This has changed. Many of the rooms where entrepreneurs are pitching their ideas are populated by lawyers or people who have grown up in the venture business with non-technical degrees. While they have a lot to bring to the decision-making, they are hard-pressed to spot a technical fraud.

The due diligence process that occurs between the pitch and the investment should go a long way to rooting out fraud, but only if it is conducted by people who can probe the data and ask the tough questions. The fraudster has prepared themselves; have the investors? Again, the list of funded frauds shows that the process has been, and continues to be, far from perfect.

Flawed Premise

Let's move on from fraud, because that is only one reason, and not the most common, that the technology doesn't work. Aside from very particular frauds, both entrepreneurs and investors must try to figure out if the entire premise on which an area of technology is based is flawed. This means that most companies proposing to solve a problem or address a market with a certain approach are doomed. How can this happen, and how can it not be obvious?

The answer is usually overhype. Hydrogen is an example that is very much current (and I know plenty of people are going to be screaming at this example!). There are many start-ups tackling the production of hydrogen, its storage, and its use in any number of applications. Governments seem to be competing with one another to talk about how the hydrogen economy is central to their energy future. When Boris Johnson was UK Prime Minister, he declared that the country would be the 'Qatar of Hydrogen.' There is no shortage of publicity about hydrogen, and no shortage of companies wanting to capitalize on that publicity to attract funding. The hype surrounding it has led to people ignoring basic problems inherent in the whole hydrogen economy proposition. These problems mean that it is hard to find any applications where hydrogen can be economically attractive without massive subsidies.

The hype behind hydrogen as the answer to a big segment of the world's energy challenges has meant that a great deal of money has been wasted, and continues to be wasted, despite application after application shown to be uneconomic. The hype was so great that it overwhelmed rational thinking and analysis, leading to numerous costly failures.

What about generative AI? Is this the most important thing to invest in for decades, is it another example of overhype that is not going to make anyone any money, or perhaps both? After the initial rush of enthusiasm, with newspaper articles and some individuals (who should know better) saying this is the end of work as we have known it, we begin to see the real possibilities as well as the limitations. The models don't continue to improve at rapid rates but seem to hit limits. Enthusiasts say this just means more processing power needs to be applied to the problem. However, the current level of processing power being applied requires huge amounts of electricity and cooling water. One can't simply say, 'Fine, I'll have ten times as much electricity and water please.' Some investors will be rushing not to miss the AI bonanza, and others will be looking at where the obvious failures are going to be because of overhype.

Despite these cautions, AI will have massive impact, across a range of difficult problems and everyday activities. We just need to be realistic about the barriers and timescales, applying a substantial discount factor to the hyped narrative. In choosing companies for investment in an area with huge hype, we must form a robust investment thesis – this is what we are going to look for and why, this is what we are not going to consider – and then stick to it. It might mean missing out on a big opportunity, but it is the only way to reduce the chance of failure when you are seeing hundreds of investment opportunities. For founders, when there is an area with large numbers of start-ups bringing forth proposals for investment, the challenge is to show that your idea is distinctive.

These are two examples of what might be a flawed premise that underlies a segment of technology. It is difficult for the investor to bring critical insight because there is so much hype around the whole area. Jumping on bandwagons is not a recipe for building big successful businesses or for venture investing. As important is that founders apply some rigorous science and engineering thinking to their proposed business at the outset to be sure that along the road to commercialization there isn't a big concrete roadblock on which it is written 'No amount of money will ever get you past this,' even if the Prime Minister says it is the greatest thing to invest in. Nobody should want to be a founder who might raise money only to spend a few precious years of their life toiling on something that is never going to work.

Scale-Up Risk: Part 1

I am going to have quite a bit more to say about difficulties in scaling up a technology from lab or pilot to full-scale deployment as a cause of failure; here

I just want to look at this from the starting point. Is there something about the technology that is not clear to either the leaders of the company or to the investor hearing the pitch, which means the technology can never be made to work? How could this happen and how could we possibly probe this?

Suppose that the company is proposing a chemical process; perhaps they are making a cosmetic component or a food additive. They have run it at lab scale, making grams of product. The product has been evaluated by some potential customers, or in the company's own laboratory, and found to be effective and safe. Having secured funding and spent several tens of millions of dollars to build a plant that can make a ton of product, they now evaluate the product, and it is found to contain traces of an ingredient that is toxic. There is no way to economically eliminate this trace product, it is inherent in the chemical pathways, and the novel chemical process, which promised either greater efficacy or dramatically lower costs, needs to be abandoned. The problem is that at gram scale this trace component is not detectable, it is effectively absent. In the 1980s, a company that I was working at had a venture to make disposable diapers (nappies for the British reader) from a crop that grew as a weed. Taking something that is seen as worthless, a weed, and making something valuable from it is the ideal venture. The absorbent properties were amazing, it seemed like a big winner. Then, when a substantial quantity of material had been made, one young woman scientist in my group tested for trace components and found a molecule that was usually harmless, unless even a very small amount of it came in contact with broken skin where it could enter the bloodstream, in which case it was fatal. It was fortunate for everyone that this venture was stopped before any babies were affected.

The same sort of thing can occur in software innovations. A program is constructed, run and shows great ability to deal with a problem. However, when the program is run a billion times, a serious error that occurs statistically once every 10 million runs, appears. Now perhaps this is something that can be fixed, perhaps it cannot. In either case, the technology as presented doesn't work.

This is an extremely hard kind of problem for both founders and investors to deal with. It is unlikely that anyone at the table can be sufficiently insightful to predict that a company will have this flaw. However, at the very least, experienced investors, especially those that have scientific or engineering experience can say, 'I have seen this movie before, and this is a risk.' They can then ask, 'Is there any way to take this risk off the table before I invest, or at least before the company has spent very much of my money?' Saying this is value additive to the founders because they are getting free advice on risks they hadn't even considered.

Scale-Up Risk: Part 2

In any chemical or energy related innovation, there will usually be several steps to go from feedstocks to products. It can be a new way of taking natural gas and converting it to a speciality chemical, or, in a company that I worked with for several years, taking coal mining waste and turning it into fuel. The key thing is that there are steps such as separation of the coal waste from rocks, washing to remove surface impurities, various physical and chemical steps, then several purification steps.

When the entrepreneurs present this process, they will show how they have done each one of these steps already and they work. Indeed, they have prepared quite a lot of the product and evaluated it, and it is efficacious. 'Now,' they say, 'What we need is enough money to build a plant that combines all these individual steps into a nice continuous process. This is minimal risk because we have already demonstrated the individual steps.'

I am going to return to discussing this sort of risk when I talk about lack of engineering, because sometimes achieving this combination of steps into a continuous process only fails because of insufficient engineering. However, here I want to present it as something that can mean that the technology doesn't work and can't be made to work. Why? Because these steps take place at different rates – some are quite quick, others are slow. When a slow step follows a quick one, the product of the first step inevitably begins to pile up, until it becomes something like the assembly line depicted in the Charlie Chaplin film *Modern Times*.

Analysis would have shown that this can never be a continuous process, and if it is a batch process, where each step is carried out separately, product stored, and then transferred into the succeeding reactor, founders and investors need to ask whether that can be made economical. The answer that sometimes comes back is that you need to do this as a slick continuous process to make money, yet that is exactly what is not possible.

There is a software analogue of this sort of problem as well. Distinct parts of a complex program, running in parallel, run at different speeds. Generally, this is not a problem, because the faster section has its results ready when the slower calculation finishes. Very occasionally, the section that is normally slower finishes before the faster, and then there are necessary inputs that cannot be found, and things spiral out of control.

Once again, having experienced engineers in the room listening to the pitch, or at least doing due diligence before investing, can avert this sort of failure or predict that it will be a potentially fatal problem.

Scale-Up Risk: Part 3

The third type of scale-up risk that makes a technology not work relates to uniformity in manufacturing. Solar cells are a good example. These are multilayered complex electronic devices that take sunlight in and get electricity out. It is not easy, but it is possible in the laboratory to make a solar cell that is about 1 cm^2 in area, and that works with high efficiency. To have a commercial product, this needs to be scaled up to at least a 1 m^2 panel, a factor of 10,000.

This has been done commercially many times, and at low cost, leading to the global solar photovoltaics industry we have today. Now someone pitches to us, 'Why stop at 1 m² panels, let's make 5 m-wide continuous rolls of solar material, and then we can just roll this out onto a rooftop, leading to a highly cost-effective electricity generator.'

'But,' say the sceptical venture capitalists, 'isn't it difficult to do that, big continuous rolls of solar material?' 'Not at all, it is just coatings, and the same thing is done for coating the inside of potato chip bags all the time.' I heard this exact question and response in California several years ago, and the reaction of the lawyers in the venture firm was, 'Oh, okay.'

Well, not okay. First, this is an electronic device, not a package for keeping the smell of potato chips from filling the supermarket. Second, it requires a degree of uniformity that is very demanding. Doing it over 1 m² is difficult yet it has been proved to be possible. Even there, the quality of output from various manufacturers varies considerably. Doing it over much greater areas is just on the other side of impossible, or it was at the time.[4] Once again, start such a company and you will spend a lot of your time and investor money trying to do the impossible.

The Technology Works (and It's Too Easy)

Suppose it is not all that challenging to get the technology to work. This could be a separate risk, but it seems a good place to end our examination of the first failure risk – the technology doesn't work. The opposite extreme is that it works, but 'it ain't that difficult to do'. The founders pitch a device that can improve the operation of conveyer belts by reducing failures and lowering maintenance costs. It is a remarkably simple thing that they invented, and they believe that the market could be enormous. Moreover, they have applied for a patent, which is likely to be granted. The improvement is dramatic, say

70 per cent lower maintenance and 10x lower failure rate, so clearly this is something we should invest in.

The only thing is, it is not just remarkably simple, it is so simple that anyone who buys one could copy it, and another manufacturer could be turning out a million of these at low cost in three months. Personally, I prefer to invest in things that are just hard enough to make so that difficulty creates a competitive barrier.

This is the conundrum – the innovation must be sufficiently difficult that the ability to make it is itself a barrier to entry for competitors or those trying to steal the technology. However, it must not be so difficult to make as to be impossible within the time and resources that will be available. Entrepreneurs need to be self-critical in assessing where they fit in this 'too easy' to 'too difficult' spectrum, but they rarely are. The job of the venture investor is to discern which of the potential investments they see is in this sweet space in between.

What Does 'Work' Mean?

Sometimes the technology works – that is, it does what the company says it will do – but that just isn't good enough to make a difference. The great venture capitalists of Silicon Valley are attracted to things that are ten times better than whatever is doing the same job now, rather than 10 per cent better. Nonetheless, we regularly hear pitches from companies that promise to revolutionize an industry, where a deeper dive shows that the improvement is much less than what is needed for a revolution.

One of the places this sort of thing pops up is in agricultural ventures ('agtech'). The pitch is that we have this material that we can spray on plants and get a 15 per cent improvement in the yield of broccoli. At the price of broccoli, cost of the spray and so on, there is a convincing story for the farmer to use our magic spray.

Digging a little deeper, we find that there is something like a standard distribution in the natural variation in broccoli yield between plants, so that one standard deviation is ±10 per cent. Once you know this, the 15 per cent improvement doesn't seem so impressive. Moreover, because of this natural variation, it is difficult for a test farm to validate the result of using the magic spray. The technology works, sort of, though maybe not well enough to make the case.

This same sort of flaw can occur in many inventions offering an incremental improvement that on first glance might seem significant, but on deeper examination is just not impressive enough. I don't mean to say that an invention that offers a 20 per cent improvement in performance is to be rejected, and only a 10x better result is worth investing in. There is currently an invention being tested that saves 1 per cent of aviation fuel consumption. Fuel is such a significant cost, and efficiencies are so hard-won, that this 1 per cent saving is material to airlines. Improvement depends on the context. The entrepreneur's job is to be able to critically assess their improvement against the question of its significance. Expect investors to be critical on this and be prepared to defend your invention. The investor's job, to reduce failure, is to have the ability to interrogate that significance in the context of industry norms.

Avoiding the Traps of the Technology That Doesn't Work

Deciding whether the technology is real, can work at scale and is a significant improvement over what is being used today, is a good place to start if we are to reduce failures. Both entrepreneurs and investors must be rigorous and analytical about this.

Investors must be constantly alert to frauds, and they come in all shapes and sizes. There can be faked data, or, 'The data will look like this when we actually get some.' Sadly, there are also liars who just want your money. Only if someone is in the room, or on the due diligence team, who can properly interrogate the entrepreneur with deep technical questions, can fraud be rooted out. The irony of completely fraudulent businesses offering step changes to existing practice is that it is sometimes the case that this breakthrough is actually possible, and someone will find a way to do it. An exposed fraud can taint a whole area, reducing the possibility of winning investment for the genuine proposition when it comes along.

Humans like to take shortcuts. Just as people cut diagonally across a lawn rather than go around a corner, scientists, especially those under pressure to produce results, show data that they have not yet actually obtained. My advice is simple. It just isn't worth it. Yes, be bold; yes, be fearless. Always be honest.

Sometimes the whole investment premise is wrong, and just because there are twenty companies chasing it doesn't mean it's going to work. Likewise, there are examples where a government, and particularly the US Government, decides it is going to put a billion dollars behind a particular technical area. Immediately people say, 'Well, with all that investment there will surely be a breakthrough.' Not necessarily! Ask someone who really takes a critical view, rather than following the hype being spread by enthusiasts. If you are an ambitious entrepreneur, think about whether you really want to be spending your time chasing this, and if you are an investor, are you about to ride a big wave onto a beach with golden sands or one with sharp rocks that will destroy your surfboard?

Lots of things work at small scale, whether in the laboratory or in a pilot software demonstration. A few of them work at large scale and only at large scale do you have a viable business. Scaling up is difficult even when it is possible, but there can be built-in reasons why a technology can never work. These can be extremely hard to see at early-stage investment, and costly to prove or disprove. Sometimes a fatal flaw is evident to an experienced investor or developer in a particular space. Founders who have asked themselves the tough questions about how the technology could fail when it is scaled up are much more impressive than those who simply wave these concerns away.

For every entrepreneur starting a business where scale-up risk is likely to be major, I would suggest that getting serious impartial analysis from an experienced engineering team is crucial. With the best of these, they will have seen the same sort of problem before and can show you just where the difficulties are going to appear. Having such teams in-house is why big chemical companies, or large manufacturers, are so successful when they scale up a process from laboratory to plant. A start-up will never have this experience or depth of talent, but they can access it in the marketplace. Sometimes, maybe often, the response will come back that this technology that worked in the lab is never going to work at scale. If you are the entrepreneur, you can either believe this and move on to doing something else, which is a difficult decision to take, or convince yourself and investors that you can overcome these difficulties. What you cannot do is simply dismiss the critique because you don't like it.

Recall that I mentioned in passing that among the Limited Partners in a venture capital fund may be 'companies that want to dip a toe into an interesting area'. These companies are sometimes known as Strategic Partners. Occasionally, a venture fund is set up in which all the partners are such companies. This is rare because it is fraught with problems of competition. On the one hand it only makes sense when the fund is going to invest in an area of mutual interest to the partners, but if they are all interested it will be difficult for them to participate openly in discussions and decisions, even in an advisory role. A more creative model is to include strategic investors in a fund where most of the money comes from family offices, pension funds and so on, with the companies investing alongside them. In this model the question of competitors is inverted, so that once one firm in a particular area comes into the fund its direct competitors are excluded. We followed this model with the CleanTech venture funds that I was involved with at Vantage Point Venture Partners.[5]

Most venture capital firms avoid courting strategic partners as fund investors, because they believe that you must spend a lot of time getting their commitment to the fund, and then they want more in the way of information than pure financial investors. This is true. I raise Strategic Partners here because they can help in avoiding failures from technology that doesn't work and can never work. Venture investors that have Strategic Partners that have tried things (and perhaps given up on them) may be able to know when, at the very least, caution is advised. When our firm was considering an early-stage investment in a process to convert biological waste material into useful fuels and chemicals using a process involving supercritical water (extremely high pressures), we reached out to designated contacts at two of our Strategic Partners. Sure enough, one of them had tried something similar, believed it was an important idea, and were able to point to several places where failure was likely to occur. In the end we did make this investment, probably because the amount of money required was small, with immense potential coupled with high probability of failure, and learned that we would indeed encounter all the problems we were warned about!

Even when the technology works, we need to ask, is this too easy so that anyone, even someone who is willing to infringe on patents, can copy it? Entrepreneurs often think about patents and trade secrets – IP – but they rarely think about this strategically. I will return to a more detailed discussion of IP strategy and what it means.

What if it does work, but the improvement offered over existing technology, while seemingly impressive, is only one standard deviation from the current approach. Effectively, that means it doesn't work well enough for anyone to be convinced that they should spend money on it. Established industries are inherently conservative and have a lot of capital invested in the way they are currently doing things. They will often do a trial of an innovative approach though rarely make a switch that involves them in both outlay of capital and increase in perceived risk. Nonetheless, if you convince one substantial player to take that risk, and the outcomes are positive, everyone will have to go along or go out of business. This entire process of disruption is going to require high levels of commitment and industry understanding on the part of the entrepreneurs, board members and advisers.

In almost all the cases I have discussed, the likelihood of these failures from the investor point of view are reduced by having scientific/engineering skills and experience in the room and on the due diligence team. Experienced scientists can quickly spot when data is faked. They also understand when something is impossible because it violates fundamental laws of physics. Experienced engineers don't just see the difficulties in scale-up, they ask the right questions that tease out when scale operation, necessary for ultimately being profitable, is impossible. Likewise, even if the right mix of skills and experience in the start-up team will not always be there or affordable, it can be accessed if there is an openness to understanding the risk that the technology will not work at scale.

It has been worth dwelling on the relatively rare fraudulent start-ups and the somewhat more common ones that are fundamentally flawed, because these are the guaranteed failures, the ones where everyone is going to waste their time, and all the money will be lost. We can now move on to more difficult causes of failure, which will start with how we find out whether as a founder you have a product that anyone will buy, at a price that allows you to make money. Not understanding the market, and what it takes to convince it to adopt your solution, is a major cause of failure that can be averted early in the life of a start-up.

REMEMBER THIS TO IMPROVE YOUR CHANCE OF SUCCESS

- ➤ When it comes to honest presentation of your company, it is fine to be bold, but you must never take ethical shortcuts, such as presenting fraudulent data or concealing damaging information.

- ➤ Frauds come in many forms, from outright frauds that steal investor money, to concealing competitors, to faking bits of data. You must have someone in the room who can ask the probing technical questions that will expose this.

- ➤ Don't get sucked into investing on the upward curve of the hype cycle. The press, and governments, can overhype areas. Investor fear of missing out (FOMO) usually leads to losing your money in these cases. If you are an entrepreneur, is your business in what is a hot area really your best idea, the one you want to spend a good chunk of your life on?

- ➤ Some technologies are just never going to work at scale. Entrepreneurs need to devote resources to trying to figure this out before a big early funding round, so that they don't waste their own precious time and other people's money.

- ➤ Ask yourself hard questions right at the start. Is this invention so easy to make that lots of people could do it? Is the improvement over current practice really meaningful, or just within natural variability?

Notes

1   'Lily Robotics', Wikipedia, https://en.wikipedia.org/wiki/Lily_Robotics, accessed 24 June 2025.

2   'uBiome', Wikipedia, https://en.wikipedia.org/wiki/UBiome, accessed 24 June 2025.

3   'Cryptocurrency Fraud – FBI', www.fbi.gov/news/stories/cryptocurrency-fraudster-sentenced-021119/, accessed 24 June 2025.

4   Power Roll, a UK company, is making progress in achieving this today with a different technical approach. www.powerroll.solar, accessed 28 June 2025.

5   https://vpcp.com.

4

The Second Cause of Failure

The Market

We have a start-up that has identified a problem and has a valid solution that they have tested at pilot scale. It's not a fraud, and so far, at least, there do not appear to be any violations of the Second Law of Thermodynamics or other easily detectable reasons why it won't work. Now will anyone buy this product?

Every start-up pitch I have ever seen has a slide on the market. They invariably show that the total available market (TAM) is something like billions of dollars, or hundreds of billions if you are a bit more aggressively optimistic, and that in just a short time the company will be able to access hundreds of millions of this huge market, and from there the sky's the limit. Still, what if the customers don't realize that they are part of the market for the magnificent innovative product that is being offered to them? There are a number of aspects of the market for a product that are causes of failure, and these can be addressed. When they are not thoroughly investigated, understood, and incorporated into the business strategy by the entrepreneurs, failure becomes the more probable outcome.

Eric Ries, in his book *The Lean Startup*,[1] addresses several ways that companies can address penetrating a market with an innovation, but his book focuses almost entirely on software products. Still, his lessons on how to make something that is good enough though not perfect, and let users try it, are valuable for all sorts of products.

How does the approach that a start-up takes (or needs to take) to the market for its product become a cause of failure? Surprisingly, perhaps, the estimate of the potential market size might be reasonably accurate, and in any case, it doesn't matter if it is $500 million or $2 billion. Most of the causes of failure relating to the market are about accessing the customers and being able to do so at an affordable cost. These customers must be educated to know they want the product. Can a start-up have the capacity and the skill to do that? With retail customers – that is, you and me – there are an awful lot of us that the company must reach. It is different if you are trying to sell your innovation to commercial or industrial customers. Business-to-business (B2B) market access is easier because there are fewer customers to educate and reach, though the targets will often be conservative and risk averse. Many industries have well-trodden routes for bringing in innovative technologies; going around those routes just won't work. Government sometimes plays a role in making the market, and the start-up will have a tough time predicting the timescale of this, often assuming incorrectly that it will be fast and certain. These and other causes of failure are explored in this chapter.

You've Got to Be Taught

Many of the most innovative products are things that consumers didn't know they needed.[2] That is not necessarily a problem, because you can start with a hundred customers – if they love the product they each tell fifty of their friends, and pretty soon you have a viable business. In many cases, however, the market must be educated.

Perhaps few of the readers of this book can remember the time before ATMs existed. To get cash from my bank account in the 1960s, I went to a branch of the bank and waited in what was usually a long slow line until I could withdraw my $100. If I forgot to get any cash before the banks closed, usually at 3 pm, I might not be able to pay my bill at a restaurant, because like most people I only had a credit card for buying fuel for my car. Thus, it might seem that everyone would welcome the arrival of a card and a machine that would dispense cash day and night.

Of course, they didn't. People were very suspicious of the security of such machines, and their accuracy. Moreover, they worried, in cities, that thieves would see them withdrawing cash and make them likely targets for mugging. It took the big banks – Barclays in the UK, Chemical and Citibank in the US – to educate consumers into liking the ATM. There was a mass market, but it had to be educated to the product. The banks had the motivation to do this – despite an upfront capital cost for the machines, they could foresee the reduction in tellers that would pay back this investment. They were using the fundamental teaching of corporations that it can sometimes be advantageous to exchange labour for capital. Probably few of them could predict the extent of branch closures.

I dwell on this because with some innovations (for example, the search engine) the quality of the product creates the market. With others, there is a lot of education, often done by advertising and direct communication with customers. Only a big organization, like Citibank or Chemical Bank in the case of ATMs, can afford to do this. Even with their backing, it took about twenty years from the time the first ATM was unveiled in 1967 until they became a common feature of consumer banking. If the start-up has a route to market through the business that is going to be doing the educating, great. But if it needs to do this itself, not so great. A cause of failure is thus that the market needs to be educated, and the start-up has neither the reach nor the resources to do the educating.

Where are we seeing innovations with this route to failure today? Anything to do with household or even small business energy use would be one area. The start-ups in this area are tackling an important problem connected with the energy transition. Some of their innovations are requiring people to use energy differently. For example, you might be asked to have a refrigerator and freezer that cannot consume electricity during the morning and evening peak hours. Now this turns out to be perfectly safe for food, yet instinctively unacceptable. Is there a utility partner, hopefully several utility partners, who are willing to take up this innovation and spend a lot of their own money educating their customers as to why it is a good thing? Once again, as with the banks, there could be a payback for the utility, because they do not have to build additional power generating capacity to cope with the peaks in demand. Once again, the start-up will never have the reach, trust, and financial wherewithal to educate the consumers itself. Failure occurs when start-ups ignore the need to educate the market.

Too Many Customers

It's not just that customers must be educated – sometimes, selling is too difficult just because of the number you must reach. Keeping to the theme of the earlier section, I have heard pitches for various innovations that can make a significant difference to the efficiency of heating a home, office or small business premises. Some of these technologies will also dramatically lower the cost of making hot water. All you need to do is install a few little widgets that connect to your gas and electricity system in the house. Seems like something everyone should want.

If a business launches with the idea that it is going to sell widgets installed in individual households, it is almost certainly going to fail. How can a small company reach all these customers, or even meet the cost of acquiring 1,000 of them? Supposing they convince 1,000 households to try the widget, it requires trained installers that will go into people's homes, every one of which is slightly different in layout. Often the installer needs to be certified to work on both gas and electricity, which very few people are. Even supposing the company does get 1,000 installations done, which seems unlikely, it must provide technical support to them, because inevitably, in the first year, things will go wrong. This technical support is just a cost because customers will expect to receive it for free. If the business is predicated on growing from selling this one product to households, their customer acquisition cost (CAC) is high, while the long-term value (LTV) of the acquired customer is low. The ratio of CAC to LTV is a critical success factor for many start-up businesses. Selling anything of this sort directly to individual households is almost a guaranteed failure of a business plan.

Still, the idea might be a good one, and it might actually offer good payback, although the individual household will struggle to do that calculation, being focused on the upfront cost. Towards the end of this book, I will talk about how we make decisions on buying something like this for our homes; for sure it is not about sitting down with a computer and doing a sophisticated calculation of the merits of the investment. Suppose instead that the same company comes with the same innovation, and says we are going to focus the first few years on selling to care homes for the elderly. Their chance of success has just gone up. There are fewer of these, but still a meaningful number. In many cases there are firms that own large numbers of care homes, so if the start-up can convince some of these to trial the innovation, and it works, then they can roll it out across their network (lower CAC). I would also be impressed if the company realizes that care homes use heat for much more of the year than private homes and probably use more hot water than a private home, so the payback is quicker.

A company (especially one that involves some sort of hardware) that goes for a large number of small customers as its initial market has a high probability of failure. Start with a small number of customers where the innovation will have a high impact, where a successful trial of the product will multiply adoption manyfold, and you have a chance of avoiding this failure.

Knowing the Route to Market

The other extreme from selling direct to individual retail customers is a start-up that has an innovation that will be sold into an established industry – vehicles, oil and gas, supermarkets, electrical utilities. This avoids the trap of too many customers. Unfortunately, it has a different route to failure.

The typical pitch for such a company when it comes to describing progress with the market is:

> We showed our invention to someone at Shell, and they allowed us to do a trial at a refinery in the Netherlands, it was very successful (you can call them to confirm) and so we believe that we will have ready acceptance across the industry. Moreover, there are just a dozen or so big players, and we can go after all of them quite economically.

The venture guys are impressed by this logic, and in doing their due diligence they speak to a technology manager at Shell, and he confirms the results that the entrepreneurs have claimed. All well and good.

But is it? What a deeper dive into one of these industry sectors reveals is that the big players never buy their technology directly from small suppliers. What they want above all is high reliability, and someone with substantial resources who will stand behind the technology. In short, they want to deal with a supplier from whom they buy numerous things and so has a lot at stake in delivering on their promises. If you are trying to sell to the oil and gas industry, this means SLB, Haliburton, Baker-Hughes, Weatherford, and a few others. In the auto industry, these are called the Tier 1 suppliers, and of the 30,000-plus parts that make up an automobile, the ones that are not made by

Ford, GM, Mercedes and so on, themselves come from Tier 1 suppliers such as Bosch, Denso, Magma, and ZF Friedrichshafen. In other words, mostly companies that the start-up and investors have never heard of. These companies in turn acquire the parts from Tier 2 suppliers, like AESIN and Berylls, and so a company trying to bring an innovation into the auto industry is effectively trying to become a Tier 2 supplier. Their customer is not Ford, GM and so on but the Tier 1 suppliers (there also exist Tier 3 companies, who are supplying the raw or nearly raw materials).

This does not make market access more difficult for these industries, it simply requires an understanding on the part of the start-up as to who their customer is, or will be, and how to access/sell to that customer. It may be that the right manager in Shell or BP or Exxon will say, 'After a trial, let me introduce you to Mr X at Haliburton, because I think they would be the company we would go to for this product.' I wish that such introductions happened more often. The truth is that the manager in the oil company probably has a lot of other things on their agenda and never thinks of making this introduction.

Even though there is no reason for industry supply structure to be a route to failure, I have seen it happen many times. Start-ups with a compelling innovation that lack understanding of how technology is adopted in an industry sector get stuck in an endless series of unpaid trials, which never lead to any significant sales before the funding runs out. Venture investors can add a lot of value if they can bring this sort of expertise to the party, and even more if they have a network of contacts in the Tier 1 suppliers or equivalent, perhaps through strategic partners.

Blame the Government

If you are interested in funding innovations in the CleanTech/Climate space, as I am, many of the pitches that you will hear rely on government doing something. Maybe it is a subsidy connected to those who build solar or wind farms, or a regulation on how much of some substance can be emitted, or how quickly companies need to reduce their emissions.

In many of these cases, it is government that creates the market, rather than free market economics. And as the prayer from the Book of Job goes, 'The Lord giveth, and the Lord taketh away.' The subsidy in place today, which underpins the business case being presented, may not be there by the time the technology is ready for mass roll-out. It may be completely gone, or it may be reduced. One party in power can feel that the key thing is to subsidize wind power, then there is an election, and the new government believes the best thing to subsidize is renewable heat. There is always a risk that a subsidy can completely disappear. One rational reason for this is that no one is using the subsidy, so government asks, why should we continue this, when it is not being taken up? That can be a matter of timing. Start-ups campaign for the subsidy based on the technology they are planning to deliver. Government responds. But instead of six months, it takes thirty months to get the technology ready. Government loses patience, assumes nothing is happening. All the technology development effort that has taken place is now not economically viable.

When I was Chair of the UK Office of Renewable Energy, we managed a large programme of subsidies. We had a clear (according to us) policy, which was that the subsidies were designed to provide those deploying the technology with a certain level of return on their sales. If we found, through our financial advisers, that the costs had come down, then we would lower the subsidy to keep the returns constant. This policy was designed to encourage the roll-out of renewables while providing fair value for money for consumers, who ultimately had to foot the bill for the subsidies. When we lowered a subsidy, there was widespread screaming, indignation, calls that we had betrayed the industry. In truth, companies had formulated and sold their business cases on the costs coming down and the subsidies staying high. The result was failures.

I don't want to imply that investors should not back businesses that require government subsidies, or regulations, to be successful. There is a good history of business being built on this basis. Government regulations can set a standard that drives innovation forward. This was discussed in a classic article by Michael Porter and Klaus van der Linde many years ago.[3] Likewise, government subsidies can take an industry that is subscale and provide the necessary support to convince investors that factories should be built, in turn driving costs down. Some countries have been remarkably successful competitively by subsidizing industries to get to scale where others are still struggling with small numbers. The investment by the Government of Taiwan in Taiwan Semiconductor Manufacturing Company is probably the outstanding example. Entrepreneurs and investors need to understand which of these two situations they are likely to find themselves in – is government a fickle partner who will promise much only to abandon you before you can succeed, or a strong backer who will help to enable your success?

If we want to avert failures in companies that require government support to get started, we need to ask tough 'what if' questions about government policy and behaviours. Moreover, and I think this is most important, entrepreneurs need to be sure that there is a pathway to profitability without government support, that the investors are convinced that such a pathway is possible, and that the company is on that pathway or will be by a defined date. Understanding that timeline, and being committed to it, tells you what your strategy needs to be for government subsidy. It can also be a powerful weapon against competitors who are behind you in a race for the market.

A Great Opportunity – and Everyone Knows It

Usually, we think about entrepreneurs as people who spot a gap in the market, a need, and have a bright idea for how to satisfy that need. Sometimes, as I've already indicated, the customers don't even know they have that need, so need to be educated. This is not the only kind of entrepreneurial activity – finding the unmet need and the clever solution.

What if several people see the same opportunity, and what differentiates them is how to best satisfy it? Edison was one of many people who saw the need for something better than gas lighting. In the world of venture investing this is more common than one might think. Some years ago, there was a lot of interest in turning waste products into useable energy in the form of heat or electricity. Which waste products, which process and how to connect the process to the market? A venture fund, such as the CleanTech funds that I was involved with, might see a company every few weeks claiming to address this problem with the optimum solution. Similarly, after Tesla attracted venture funding as a start-up electric vehicle company, there were many others rushing into the space, some offering small vehicles, or vans, or construction equipment, as well as some that were direct copies of Tesla's initial target of electric sports cars.

The job of the venture investor is to back the company that stands out from the rest in this sort of crowded space. Putting money behind the tenth best company out of 100 is not going to give you great odds for success. Easy to say – if you want to avert failure, back the best company – but hard to do.

I include this under market-related causes of failure, though it could fit in other places, because the starting point for both entrepreneurs and investors is likely to be an understanding of what the market sees as the problem. For example, if the universe of companies being considered is technology for finding and stopping leaks of poisonous, or explosive, or greenhouse gases, what are the customers asking for? Is it detection limits (how small a leak can you find)? Perhaps for most customers the priority is the lowest cost solution even if it is not the most sensitive. Some customers may want the solution that has the lowest labour costs for operation. There are a number of things that will differentiate among the 100 companies trying to capture this market. It is the job of the entrepreneur to convince investors that their solution is the best, while it is the job of the investor to evaluate this claim. The only way you can know which is the best solution, the most investable, is by figuring out which is the second best, third best, and so on, and why.

This starts with the market, then it goes far beyond that. Sometimes the classic adage applies, 'The best is the enemy of the good.' A company might have something that is the most sensitive and even has the potential to be the cheapest. Unfortunately, it is technically so complex that it can't be brought to market soon enough. Other solutions, with perhaps less capability, come to market, are sold and adopted, and then the better solution has to displace them, which is often nearly impossible. You must convince the customer that they made a mistake.

I am always impressed when I sit in a meeting with other investors and hear, 'Companies, A, B, C, and D are tackling this problem, which we all agree is going to be a big business. We like C, because it does this better than A, and these things make it better than B and D, and we hear signals from the market that confirm this view.' Even better is when the founders have considered the market and the competitors with sufficient critical thinking, which is evident when they present this analysis.

From my experience, investors need time to develop this sort of viewpoint and understand which is the best company in a space. The most sophisticated venture funds identify an area, like waste to energy, and begin to follow the companies trying to make a success in this market. They talk to potential customers to understand the drivers behind their purchasing decision. They evaluate the CEOs and Chief Technology Officers (CTOs) of the companies in the space to see how well they understand the market they are trying to access. Gradually they put together a grid with the key criteria for success, and the companies vying for the market, with an evaluation of each. If they are lucky, one or two stand out from the rest. If there is no standout, perhaps there is a deeper problem. Some of those deeper problems are explored under other causes of failure.

All this is the rational approach. I wish I could say that in my time in venture investing I saw the rational approach as the one that was always (even mostly) used to select investments. Unfortunately, it was not. The culture of the 'rock star founder' is always present. Three different entrepreneurs have come in and given well-argued and scientifically backed-up presentations about how they are going to tackle a particular market need. Then in comes someone who led another Silicon Valley company, often led it to failure rather than 'grand slam' success, but they are well known and a great talker. Whoosh. That's the sound of rational thinking going out the door into the California sunshine as the partners rush to give this person the money. Another failure has just been added to the portfolio.

If you are investing from a big fund, say hundreds of millions of dollars, it is not just the early round investments that you have to consider, and the follow-on rounds from the investments you have made. You will also have opportunities to invest in B, C and later rounds of companies. Suppose that you invested in one company in the waste to energy space, it probably means that you passed on several others because you thought they were not as good. Now comes the possibility that one of the ones that you thought was second or third best is making good progress, and you are approached about coming in, at a higher valuation, in the B round. Do you just say no, we already decided against them? Or do you listen to the story again, and evaluate their progress, comparing it to the company you did invest in? Arrogance says pass, competence says listen.

Just as big companies spend a lot of time understanding the structure of their industries – who are the major players, who are the upstarts, what are our own strengths and weaknesses – it is important for start-up companies to do the same. Rigorous competitor analysis always pays off, so not doing it increases the risk of failure. For the start-up space, understanding the landscape of investors, knowing who is backing which of your competitors, even knowing when they are unhappy with their decision, is additional intelligence that can be a competitive edge.

The Problem of Getting Others to Stand Still

The entrepreneurs from Fast Tomatoes come to us and say, 'Today the yield of tomatoes in greenhouses is x, and we can achieve a 20 per cent improvement, and the growers tell us that is material. We get that by applying our magic coating to the greenhouse.' 'But,' we say to them, 'there is already a magic coating sold by another company, Hot Tomatoes, isn't there?' 'Yes,' they say triumphantly, 'our 20 per cent improvement is compared to the yield with the existing coating sold by Hot Tomatoes.'

So that looks fine, or does it? The entrepreneurs will need a fair amount of capital and some good partnerships to get their product proven and scaled up. They estimate it will take three years – realistically we know it will probably take five. Still, a 20 per cent improvement, which our market due diligence says is worth going for. What's wrong with this picture?

Over at Hot Tomatoes, an established player, there is also a research lab. And there they are constantly working to improve their coatings. Six months after we invest in Fast Tomatoes, Hot Tomatoes releases a new product that halves the improvement our investment was able to deliver. Moreover, they have thousands of customers to whom they can market the new product.

This development spurs on our entrepreneurs, rather than discourages them, and they find a way to squeeze yet more improvement out, even though this delays the commercialization by six months. And in a year, Hot Tomatoes brings out yet another product.

Never assume, when there is an existing product in the market that you are trying to displace, that your competitors will stand still. Your challenge spurs them on, and they have some built in advantages. It doesn't mean that you will inevitably lose. Of course not. The Welsbach Mantle, which produces a steady intense glow from gas lights, was invented after Edison's electric light bulb. It was a marked improvement over flickering flame gas lamps, yet electric lighting still triumphed. All I am saying is be conscious of what your assumptions are, and if one of them is that there are competitors who will not improve, that is reason for asking some tough questions if you want to reduce the chances of working on or investing in a failure.

What We Learn to Do and Not to Do to Deal with the Market

The big lesson if you want to avoid these routes to failure is to have a deep understanding of the market you are trying to access. Too many founders concentrate on estimating the size of the accessible market, probably because it makes them feel like they can build a big business without taking an unreasonable share, and because they know this is something potential investors want to hear about. To be successful, I would assert that you should spend very little of your effort on the size of the market, and a lot of it on the structure of the market. Let's pick this apart for different cases.

Now it may be that you are trying to displace an existing product, in which case things are both easier and more difficult. They are easier because it is possible to know who has this product, what they love or hate about it, how much they have to pay to replace it if it is coming to the end of its life, what problem is it solving and what problems it does not solve. If someone is a potential customer for the existing product, but hasn't bought one, what is holding them back? Perhaps most important, how difficult and how costly will it be for an existing user to switch from the competitor to your product? Even if your solution is better, these switching costs can be a major barrier that will keep it from being adopted. At the same time, you will want to be building switching costs into your solution. Only by understanding the market can you feed back to your product development team what would be effective in terms of switching costs.

Related to switching costs with an existing market are network economies. The technology developments of the past quarter century have shown us just how powerful it can be for a product to become the dominant one in a market where users are in constant communication with one another. Even when it is not Facebook, a networked game or a messaging app, there can be less visible network economies. You would be wrong to think that having one dominant model of clothes washer doesn't necessarily offer any network economies. It means that the manufacturer can supply spare parts better than small competitors, train service personnel and maintain a service network that gives fast response. As with switching costs, network economies can be a barrier to adoption of your product, while building network economies into your scale-up creates a competitive barrier. I will return to both switching costs and network economies towards the end of the book when I discuss strategic thinking for start-ups.

Things are quite different when you are providing a solution to a problem that your potential customers may not even know they have. How many of us knew that we needed our phones to count the number of steps we take each day? When technology is evolving rapidly, there will be many such markets, as we know from the apps that continue to appear on our phones. There needs to be a way for founders to test the market for such products, and these tests come with a caution – the individuals, maybe also the businesses, that are willing and eager to try the new product may be far from typical of the average user that you need to capture if you are going to build the business to scale. Still, you must start someplace, even if you need to be cautious about generalizing market acceptance and CACs from your first enthusiastic trial users.

One way of looking at the market issues described in this chapter is how many decisions need to be made for the company to achieve meaningful revenue. I will deal with industries with a limited number of influential customers below. If it is a government regulation mandating your solution, then perhaps it is one decision, for example government requires every company making a particular product to keep its emissions of certain pollutants to less than x parts per million. This is one decision; however, it can be a difficult one for a start-up to influence. If there is a strategic investor with a big stake in getting the market to happen, and they are willing to use their influence with government(s) to put the rule in place, that could be a significant competitive boost leading to successful growth. Even if you have government regulation mandating your product, this is likely to lead to many competing companies providing something similar. In this case, who wins? Having regulations narrowly written is the best route to success. Being first to market can be a big advantage. Being cheapest, even if not best, will certainly be attractive to many customers who want to comply with the regulations at the lowest possible cost.

The opposite extreme is that success means selling to individual retail customers. There are two things you must do. First, the customers have to be educated, sometimes to know that they have the problem your company is solving. Second, they have to believe that your solution is safe and desirable. Ultimately, if a company can afford to do this, and has the skills to do it, the win can be enormous (witness Apple, Google, Eli Lilly (Mounjaro), etc.). Have the founders and investors appreciated up front that this is the market model, and is there a clear route to dealing with what is required to achieve scale in this market? As many writers of start-up advice have said, get a product out there, let people use it, take their feedback, make it better, try it on more people, complete this virtuous loop. Don't worry about growing at breakneck speed at first, because if you have something really good then accelerated growth will happen. In short, we build understanding of the market by doing experiments and learning from the results, something smart retailers have done for generations. We also know that building a business takes time, and resources need to be adequate to support that time for market understanding.

In between is B2B sales. Perhaps this is easier, as there are fewer customers than with a direct retail market, and often some of them are so influential that if you get them to use your product, others will follow. The crucial thing here is understanding how new technology comes into these established industries – be it software, energy, automotive, whatever. Often it is through the so-called Tier 1 suppliers. These suppliers to big companies meet with them regularly, discussing technology problems and desired solutions. Often these dialogues will be along the lines of, 'if we could reduce the cost of converting A to B by 30 per cent, it would open up a huge new business for us, and we wonder if it might be possible by …'. Hearing this, the Tier 1 suppliers are turning to existing technology providers and issuing the same sort of challenge. These suppliers effectively have the valuable market information you need to access the B2B customer, and the successful start-up will build the relationship that gives them that exact information. I emphasize again that start-ups can get the research departments of a Ford, Exxon, or Duke Energy to try something, but that is not going to get the sales job done. Only the supplier industry can do that. When I talk to founders, it is a sign of sophistication in a start-up that they have taken the trouble to develop a deep understanding of the way new technology is adopted in the industry they are trying to penetrate, and then use this understanding to their advantage.

Selling to businesses requires patience and persistence. A business customer, even one who has bought your product through a Tier 1 supplier, usually wants to spend some time doing a trial to see if it really does work as well as claimed. Depending on the nature of the product, the trial might throw up questions. Can you generate a report in this format? Will you be able to integrate into our data management system? What level of cyber security have you built in? Responding to these questions, especially with an important customer of the Tier 1 supplier, takes time and probably some additional effort. It's worth it because other big customers are likely to want the same thing. Then, having eventually completed the trial successfully with an upgraded product, the B2B customer decides that they want to place an order. First, however, they need to put this through internal systems to agree that they are going to change the way they are doing things. Then they may have to wait until the next budget cycle to secure the funding to buy your product. Depending on market structure, you might need to jump through several hoops with the procurement department to become an approved supplier to the customer. All of this takes time – not days or weeks but months or years. The company leadership and the board need to appreciate just how long and how costly all this will be if you are trying to penetrate such a market. Only then can you produce a realistic financial plan, with the company funded appropriately.

Finally, investors must be conscious of the other players trying to access the same market, or those who are already providing a solution to a problem which, while (you are convinced) it is not as good, already has traction with the leading companies. Are we investing in the best start-up of those going after the market? Can we say which is the second, third, fourth best company? As time goes on, are investors keeping an eye on the competitors to see if they are progressing more rapidly than our company, or are we opening the gap on them? If the former, are we prepared to switch horses? Both investors and founders need to assume that competitors, particularly those with existing market position, will not stand still in the face of our challenge. They will always be trying to close the gap just as we are trying to widen it.

We increase our chances of success when start-ups take the time and put in the effort to have a deep understanding of the market, how it is structured, and what are the access points. A lot of this can be done up front, rather than when you are two years into developing and test marketing your product. That is why I have put this as the second cause of failure.

We have technology that is genuine, and we have reasonable cause to believe it will work at scale. Now we have done a thoughtful assessment and developed an understanding of the market, do we have the skills to actually make this product?

REMEMBER THIS TO IMPROVE YOUR CHANCE OF SUCCESS

- Have a deep understanding of the market you are trying to access. Too many founders concentrate on estimating the size of the accessible market; and spend very little of their effort on the size of the market, and a lot of it on the structure of the market.

- If you are trying to displace an existing product, find out what its users love or hate about it, how much they have to pay to replace it if it is coming to the end of its life, what problem is it solving and what problems it is not solving. If a potential customer hasn't bought the existing product yet, what is holding them back?

- How difficult and how costly is it to switch from the competitor to your product?

- Selling to big business? Understand how new technology comes into these established industries and find your way down that route. It always takes longer than expected to get big companies to make a buying decision.

- Be conscious of the other players trying to access the same market, or those who are already providing a solution which, while not as good, already has traction with the leading companies.

Notes

1. Eric Ries, *The Lean Start-Up* (New York, NY: Crown Business, 2011).
2. Henry Ford's famous quote was, 'If I had asked people what they needed, they would have said a faster horse.'
3. Michael E. Porter and Claas van der Linde, 'Green and Competitive', *Harvard Business Review*, 73, no. 5 (September–October 1995): 120–34.

5

The Third Cause of Failure
Missing Engineers

I was listening to a pitch in California from a team with a process to turn a biological fermentation by-product into a valuable fuel or chemical. They had carried out a series of systematic and well-executed experiments that showed that the proposed process was very efficient, convinced us that there was a huge market for the product of their process, and now 'all they needed to do' was scale it up. Two years from now they could have a working demonstration plant, and in another year or two a full-scale plant. The team consisted of three chemists and two business development people.

As we turned to questions, I said, 'Look, this is interesting. I think it is going to take quite a lot of engineering to scale it up, and you guys are not engineers.' Their response was very enlightening: 'That's why we are seeking funding. As soon as this capital raise is in place, we will hire an engineer.'

An engineer! This shows just how naive scientific founders can be. I could not resist saying,

> Look, if DuPont was at your stage with a new process and they decided to scale it up to commercial size, they would put together a team of about 100 engineers, maybe more, which would include chemical engineers, mechanical, controls, safety, and others. And the quality of every one of those engineers would be better than anyone you would be likely to hire.

Even start-ups that turn into highly successful companies can start out naive in this regard. When the founders of an electric car start-up made a pitch to our venture fund for its first funding, they had built one car. They did this by taking the body of a sports car, and replacing the engine with about 700 computer batteries wired together. It worked and it was very impressive in its performance. And this was a group of guys who had built successful companies in Silicon Valley, so they had credibility, even fame.

At the end of the presentation, one of my partners said, 'Look, you are heroes of Silicon Valley, but do you know anything about building cars?' And the response was, 'Me and my friends here, we built the internet. How hard could it be to build a f***ing car?'

Well, it's not hard to build one car, as they had shown. It is hard to build thousands or millions of cars. To build a manufacturing line that produces cars with uniformly high quality, which meet government safety regulations so they can be certified as roadworthy. They needed expertise to develop the supply chain for all the parts that would go into the millions of cars – something completely different from the expertise required to build a software company. The company's founders had none of this capability; however, they soon realized that they needed it, because they were sophisticated business founders with a powerful vision of disrupting the entire market for personal road transport. They attracted substantial funding, so they could hire great experienced engineers from General Motors, Ford and others.

One of the most frequent causes of failure is severely underestimating the **quantity** and **quality** of engineering required to go from prototype, lab, even the first release of a software product, to something that is commercially successful at scale. Earlier, I talked about scale-up problems inherent in the technology that predestined failure. Now I want to explore failure that doesn't have to happen if the resources and approach to scale-up are done properly.

Engineering: That's The Name of the Game

Many years ago, I read an article in *Forbes* magazine entitled Why CEOs Fail.[1] The essential message was this: It's not strategy, it's execution. Is this true for start-ups as well as big companies? Yes and no. Strategy is important, and too often ignored by start-ups and their boards. Nonetheless, without the ability to build your product, over and over again, better and better, you don't have a business. The legendary Silicon Valley investor John Doerr said, 'Ideas are easy, execution is everything.'[2] It takes engineering, and plenty of it, to execute on product delivery.

Once we get past the failures caused by technology that doesn't work, we have learned that the market is not only there and the route to access the market is understood, the company still must execute on making the product. Maybe this is going from a process demonstrated at lab scale to a first plant, which could be one that's only one-tenth the size of a full-scale commercial plant – still a hundredfold increase in scale from the lab. It can be the transition from making two devices and getting them out for testing to being able to make one a day, every day, en route to a production line where hundreds a week can be made and delivered to customers. Or it can be delivering a full software package that copes with the variety of user sophistication, while supplying all the features that key customers demand. This after showing more limited capability to a small number of your first patient customers.

It doesn't matter what sort of start-up technology business you are in – it is only by having great engineering capability that you will be able to make this transition from prototype to commercial product. Time after time I have seen how the start-up company underestimates the quantity and range of engineering expertise that is required. Just as telling is that the venture investors also underestimate this.

It is easy to see why most entrepreneurs are prone to failing in their appreciation of the quantity and quality of engineering needed. A lot of start-up ideas come from scientists, even if they are working at the applied end of their scientific discipline. The education of a scientist is quite different from that of an engineer. Assuming they have been to one of the better universities in the world, scientists and engineers have had their young brains rewired. The outcome of that rewiring is not at all the same for the scientist as it is for the engineer. As a result, the scientist does not see the importance of design, while the engineer sees that as the centre of their discipline. Making something novel and important that works in the laboratory can be extremely difficult; the scientist that achieves this thinks, 'Okay, just turn it over to the engineers now to make it happen at scale.' Their education has not taught them anything about what that entails, or even how to think about what it entails. As a result, they underestimate both the challenge and the resources required.

Why would supposedly sophisticated investors not see this clearly? As usual, it is about what you know and don't know, but in Silicon Valley it is also about arrogance – thinking you know all about building a technology business even if you have never done so and have limited technical education. While everyone can see the customer facing design features of any product, much of what engineers have done to make the product happen with high reliability, safety, at low cost, efficient in consumption of power is invisible to both the customer and to the investors. That is why they don't recognize its importance.

The system encourages the entrepreneurs to underestimate the difficulty and time needed to go from where they are (lab, prototype) to commercial product, because if they are too honest, they don't get funded. If the founders are scientists, they may be almost as ignorant as the lawyers they are talking to in the investor firm about what it takes. The expertise is not in the room for the potential investors to say,

> Ok, you have asked for this amount of money, and you say you will use it to hire x, y and z, from which you will deliver $$$$ by 2026. What we know,

from experience, that what you need is three times that amount of money, to hire 3x, 7y, as well as q, r, and s, and if everything works perfectly, you will deliver $$ by 2027. By the way, actually delivering that smaller amount of money with a bigger staff would be an exceptionally good result!

At the same time, there is no encouragement for the entrepreneurs to say, even if they knew this, that 'We have a big and difficult job ahead, and we are the guys who can do it. With the funding we are raising, we will develop our currently almost non-existent engineering department into one that can deliver products/processes on time and on budget, with high reliability.' The founders know that their audience would rather hear unjustified optimism than educated realism. This combination of ignorance and arrogance about engineering challenges and resources can be fatal.

A Range of Problems

For any of the scale-ups I've described, there are going to be a range of engineering problems to be solved. A company makes devices that have complex optical and electronic components that are sealed in a tube with an optical window at one end. The devices operate outdoors and need to work at temperatures from -40 to +50°C. For the first couple of prototypes the window could be carefully sealed by hand using a thin strip of glue. Once we start making one a day, those seals really need to be reproducible and perfect. This means the window and its mount need to be redesigned and a robotic sealing process implemented. It's a critical element, probably the most mundane in this extraordinarily complex device, still it is a step in the manufacturing process requiring a couple of skilled engineers to design and implement. Now, for this one device, there were probably more than 100 engineering problems of this sort that needed to be professionally solved to go from prototypes to production, requiring sophisticated electrical engineering, optical engineering, safety, and many more engineering skills.

In trying to scale up a chemical process, which will usually involve several steps including mixing, reactions, sometimes catalysts, separations, possibly drying, there may be fatal flaws that mean the technology can never work. More often, the problems are there but they are not necessarily fatal. Sure, there are fast steps and slow steps in the process; that is always the case, and most of the time engineers can analyse the problem, decide that it is solvable, knowing what sort of hardware and controls need to be put in place to deal with this. This is one example of the myriad problems, some small, others complex, that an experienced person solves in a day, while occasionally one requires a team of designers to figure out the solution. There are just a lot of these sorts of challenges, and they each demand a different range of engineering expertise.

Great engineers will solve problems they have never faced before, but problems will be solved a lot quicker if the engineer sees something that they have already experienced so knows just how to take care of it. When DuPont or BASF decides to scale up a process developed in its laboratories, it has the experience of having done this many times, which means it can usually anticipate what will occur. There is a range of engineering talent in-house that it can supplement as needed from external firms to solve process problems as they appear during design, construction, and commissioning of the plant. By contrast, the challenges for the start-up are twofold – it must anticipate the kind of problems that will occur, and be sufficiently attractive to engineers, who are usually in high demand, to assemble the team of people capable of solving these problems in order to make the process work at scale.

Both challenges are difficult but surmountable. The first step is having entrepreneurial leadership and investors that recognize that the challenge actually exists, and in my experience a lot of the failures are caused by this not being the case. In effect you are asking leadership to appreciate that there will be difficulties in getting to scale before they have occurred. Once you have this recognition, both the company and its investors must act on it, spending the money on the people with the experience to solve these (not yet arisen) problems. Too often the founders don't know what they don't know, and the same is true for the investors. They are biased towards optimism, so when problems do occur, they are unprepared to solve them, even though they are soluble problems. The result? Certainly considerable delay, which may cause failure because you run out of money; frequently failure because the expertise is just not there to solve the problem(s).

A Range of Engineering Disciplines

When a start-up founder says, 'No problem, we are going to hire a couple of engineers,' it means that they have no idea what engineering is, what engineers do, or the range of problems they are going to be faced with.

Historically, most nineteenth–twentieth-century engineering programmes at major universities, including the specialized engineering universities, were built around the disciplines of civil, mechanical, chemical and electrical engineering. All of these require strong fundamental education in mathematics and physics.

As engineering has evolved, while these four disciplines have endured, there are many subdisciplines and specialisms that have also become part of engineering education and practice. Environmental, safety, computer hardware and software, controls, manufacturing, project management, bioengineering... there is a lengthy list. In all cases engineers learn about design because that is fundamental to what they do, applying that competency in design to the specialist area in which they have deep knowledge.

The need for these engineering disciplines and special areas of expertise pervades many of the plans for development of start-up businesses that pitch to venture capitalists. Probably everyone recognizes that software is going to be needed, only those who have experienced it will appreciate how difficult it is to get software to be flawless and able to meet customer requirements. Less appreciated are things like controls, the hardware and software that keep a process running smoothly, producing quality product, week in and week out. Professionally designed controls help to minimize the personnel required to keep the plant running, so they make the entire process more economically attractive. There are many other things of this sort. Let me highlight just one – cost estimation.

Before the first reaction vessel or computer is ordered, before any concrete is poured as a base for something to be installed upon, there must be engineers who will determine what it is all going to cost. Has the start-up team ever heard of the discipline of cost engineering, or estimating engineering? While this is not a usual degree that an engineer obtains, it is often included as a sub-specialism in civil engineering or construction engineering courses, though many engineers will, at either the undergraduate or master's degree level, take a course covering the basics of cost estimation.

All capital costs are estimates, to varying levels of precision and certainty. For the investor, if there is a device to be made or a pilot plant, or, longer term, a full-size plant, the projected cost will be a key factor in determining three things: Will my investment be sufficient to get us to the next stage? When we get to full-scale production, will the capital costs be low enough to achieve an advantage over competitive approaches to the same problem? If we are successful, will the capital and operating costs be low enough so that we will, at some point in the future, be able to make money from this product or process?

I have often seen entrepreneurs present such costs without any idea of the level of uncertainty of their estimate. They say things like, 'We can build this plant for $24.7 million.' By contrast, if you were in a big company, with sophisticated project cost estimation, you would hear, 'At the current stage of our work, we estimate that the cost is $25 million ±30 per cent.' In a recent angel investment that friends of mine made, they relied on a cost estimate from the entrepreneurs to build a device, which, before they had even started to build it, went up by 50 per cent. What this means is that the company has raised money to build a first set of devices to test the market for their innovation, and before they have even started, they do not have the money to carry out their plans. Failure prevention requires strong and careful interrogation of cost estimates.

Engineering Quality

It is not just that there are a wide range of engineering problems to be solved, requiring a diverse set of disciplines and specialities. There is also the question of the quality of the engineers. A few years ago, I was working with a company that was building a first-of-a-kind plant in the US. The company was a start-up, and while the CEO did not have process plant expertise, there were certainly people in the company who did. There was a substantial, local, engineering firm contracted to do the construction and commissioning of the plant, eventually handing it over for commercial operation. From the very beginning there were problems, some in the design, and many in the ability of the engineers in the firm to deal with challenges as they came up. Another director and I brought in a senior engineer from his firm to look at things and report to us. His verdict: With the quality of people doing the work, what was planned as a three-month job commissioning the plant was unlikely to be completed in less than a year. This advice was met with outrage and scorn. Sure enough, one year later the plant was still not operating at more than 50 per cent of capacity.

One of my mentors was a great electrical engineer, the late Professor Athanasios Papoulis, author of many books and papers, and someone who taught several generations of young, successful engineers. In one conversation we had, he told me about how the quality of engineering education shows up as a distinction between engineers who have great careers and those who don't. Many engineers are taught how to solve certain kinds of problems – they learn formulas and methods, and as long as those are relevant, they are capable of earning a living. As technology advances, the problems change, the tools change, the solutions change, and these engineers become obsolete. 'What I do,' he said, 'is teach my students how to learn new things, and that is what makes them valuable for many years.'

Nowhere is this more evident than in the engineers who work in start-ups. The more revolutionary the technology, the more likely that the day-to-day activity of the engineer is solving problems that have not been seen before, none of which were taught in undergraduate lectures or laboratories. It is essential that a start-up has the quality of engineering talent that can tackle such problems. The cause of failure is rarely that the problem is unsolvable or too difficult to solve in time. It is more often that the engineer given the task is not up to the job.

Location can help. In almost every country, except for very small ones, engineering talent is not distributed evenly across geography. There are always regions where there are a lot of engineers (and of course a large number of companies employing them), and other regions with very few. Start-ups will have a better chance of success in recruiting both the quantity and quality of engineers they need if they are located in one of these regions.

High-quality engineers are also not afraid to move from one company to another, because they know that they will be in demand. Some years ago, I was chair of a company that was making a radical change in direction, and as a result some fifty engineers were going to be losing their jobs. I was very worried about them and their families, at the same time knowing that the company did not have the resources to do much for them in the transition. My fears were unfounded, because we were in the broad geographic area of technology business around Cambridge in the UK, and every one of the engineers had new jobs offered to them very quickly. By choosing the location of your start-up carefully, you have a better chance of getting the engineering talent you need to avoid failure.

Get Someone Else to Do It for You

Many times, when I question entrepreneurs about the lack of engineers on their team, the response is, 'Not a problem, we are going to use Super Duper Contract Engineering in Ireland to do this for us.' In other words, there is a problem, we have recognized the problem, and we are going to pay someone to solve it for us.

Now at some level this is a sensible approach. Suppose you have designed a device, perhaps made five prototypes and had them evaluated, now you need the capability to make 10,000. It may well be that someone else has that capability, and it would take you years to build it up yourself. Indeed, a good creative contract engineering and manufacturing firm will show you how to take your prototype and redesign it so that it is manufacturable at scale. As part of this engagement, they will make your device smaller, lighter weight, more robust, and ultimately cheaper. They will also help you with suppliers of components. Doesn't this sound like a really good answer to the engineering resource challenge I have posed?

The answer to that is yes and no. These contract engineering firms will have to invest a lot of time and effort up front to get your device designed. What they need to be convinced of is that the market is going to be very large. The problem is that so far you have built five, sold two, and project that next year it will be 1,000, which the contract manufacturer will discount to 100. The challenge is to get the attention of a good firm at this early stage.

What often happens is that, getting no response from one of the top tier firms, start-ups turn to small firms in their geographic area. These firms will promise anything to get their hands on your money (actually the investors' money); unfortunately, delivery is often very weak. Even in these firms, how much of their attention you get depends on whether they believe that the first contract could lead to bigger things in the future. In my experience, the quality of output is often satisfactory, by which I mean a device that works and can be built in larger numbers, but that is not extraordinary in terms of performance, higher specifications, supply chain, cost, and perhaps most important, reliability. You need extraordinary engineering on all these things. The worst problem with the smaller firms is timeliness. They are scrambling between contracts, trying to keep several people happy, and inevitably everything is late. Start-ups burning through cash cannot afford delays.

The same sort of problem comes with outsourcing the engineering connected to building a process plant. You have built a pilot plant, or have proven that each step of a process can be carried out at reasonable scale, but now have to integrate the entire process into a continuous operation. You want a big engineering firm to do this for you. Can you get the attention of a firm such as Jacobs, WSP Global or AECOM? They will have the capability to do it; once again they need to be convinced that there are going to be many more plants like the first one, because that is how they will make their money. They will also worry that you may run out of money before the job is done, while they have blue chip customers who are asking for projects with lower risk on all fronts, even though the large customers will squeeze them on price. Once again you turn to a smaller, more local, less capable firm, and we return to the problems described in the previous paragraph.

In both cases, devices or process plant, there needs to be a strong in-house engineering capability to work with the contractor. This is not a case of, 'Throw it over the fence and let them build it, then take possession.' Designing for manufacture is an iterative process that the start-up must be able to take part in as the key technical partner. This participation will only happen if the engineering expertise is present within the company, at least in a small, highly competent, core team.

Getting Quantity and Quality of Engineers Right First Time

Engineering starts with design and continues with problem solving. Chemists, physicists, biologists invent reactions, devices or drugs. It is engineers who design products that can be manufactured. Engineers transform chemical reactions into chemical processes. Engineers build things that work reliably day in and day out, so that a business develops a reputation for quality. It really doesn't matter if the product is a massive chemical plant or a tiny device inside your phone that tracks how many steps you have taken, if it is a drug that helps you lose weight or a computer program that produces four-dimensional spreadsheets. All of them must be designed so that they can be manufactured in large quantities and function with high degrees of reliability.

Businesses that succeed do all of this, they do it at a cost that is attractive to the customer while also making a sufficient margin to pay all the costs, still having enough left over to reward investors. To restate this, in business you are trying to answer the question, 'If we can get everything to work, can we sell it at a cost that will be attractive to the customer, and still allow us to make money, not at first, but at least eventually?' The entire process of going from lab or basement to a big business is about engineering; if you want your company to succeed you will recognize this from the outset, plan for it and hire accordingly.

As we have become a deeply technological society, and remember that this is very much a 125-year-old – therefore relatively recent – development, so our standards for reliability of our technology have increased. In the 1950s, when cars were concluding their first half-century of mass manufacture, they still broke down for various reasons. I am old enough to remember that it was usual on a 100-mile journey to see a few cars by the side of the road along the way with a flat tyre, broken fan belt, overheated radiator. People expected it and tolerated it. This rather unexceptional level of reliability was achieved, despite a requirement for new cars being serviced by the dealer every 1,000 miles and having an oil change every 2,000 miles. The next twenty years saw a massive change in automotive reliability. For many decades now, we do not expect our car to break down for any reason, and it rarely does. Cars are serviced once a year, and that is probably more for the good of the dealership than of the car. Oil is usually filled once for the life of the car. Automobiles, which are now much more complex than they were seventy-five years ago, have been engineered to incredible standards of reliability. In our technological society, this higher expectation of performance has become pervasive, though of course with every new product there is a period of progression to high reliability. We all experienced this with our first few personal computers, and still experience it with devices that, for some reason, occasionally need to be unplugged and plugged back in again five minutes later because some fault has occurred. All innovative technologies have learning curves, but they are getting shorter. The result is that the customers for your start-up have come to expect high reliability in every bit of technology you sell them. Building a business that grows and succeeds comes from having the engineering talent to achieve these exacting standards of reliability.

Inventors devise the first thing of a kind. No one has ever made one before. That is why it is an invention. Designing for manufacture of inventions means engineering in simplicity and removing complexity, ensuring ruggedness, because users drop things and use them at extreme temperatures, while always, always looking for ways to reduce cost. None of this must be done at a sacrifice to reliability. Achieve all of this and your chance of success goes way up.

Even after all the design is done, a plant must be built to manufacture. This might be pretty benign, if what you are building is software or assembling some electrical components and putting them in an attractive package. Or it could be the opposite extreme if you are building a plant to manufacture hydrogen cyanide. No matter what, the first step is getting permission to do this from local authorities, which generally involves finding ways to ensure that the environmental impact will be minimized, with the obligation on the company for proving just what that impact will be. It may go beyond impact on air, water and land. How much electrical power does the plant need, and what happens if that power is interrupted? There are hundreds of questions that need to be competently answered. That is why we have a whole subdiscipline of environmental engineering. Is the ground suitable for the weight of equipment that is going to be placed on it; what foundations are needed? Civil engineering and its subdiscipline, geotechnical engineering, answers those questions. I have already mentioned costing and controls, and much more. Of course, not everything works perfectly the first time. Skilled engineers solve these problems, remove bottlenecks, while continuing to reduce costs and increase product uniformity.

Every founder and every investor looking to the future of their technology business must be asking the tough questions about where the engineering is going to come from to meet these challenges. This is fundamental, and it cannot be waved away as something 'We will just get done' or 'We will outsource.' Being conscious of the quality and quantity of engineering that is going to be required, planning for what is needed, acting on that plan – this is what distinguishes companies that can succeed from companies that do succeed. Michael Porter has written about the powerful role played by geographic clusters,[3] places where many technology firms are located. These are the areas where engineers live, and often where some of the best contract design firms are located as well. The importance of clusters in the context of a technological start-up is that your chance of success is increased if you are located in or near one of them.

Founders emerge from the laboratory or the garage with a business idea that they have tested in a very preliminary fashion. Fine. But if you want to succeed there needs to be at least one person on the leadership team, preferably also one among trusted and respected senior advisers, who both believes in the product and knows what it takes to get your product from where you are today to where you need to be two years from now. That person will have deep education and experience in engineering. They will help with understanding the price at which you will be able to sell the product at first and ultimately. That is the crucial piece of prediction that says whether this invention can ever be a viable business. They will also suggest contract firms with whom you might be able to partner during the process of scaling up. If they are board members or advisers who are respected by the industrial community, they will be able to reach out to contract firms and persuade them to at least look at the possibility of giving your company high quality engineering support.

If you are a scientific founder, you will believe the numbers, the timetable and the resource requirements that your own engineering team and your advisers tell you, because they have gone through the same thing with one or more companies. These requirements will be built into your funding plan. It may well be that this makes it look like it will take longer than you would like to get to the point where you are producing sufficient commercial product to test the market, and still longer to get to a full-scale plant that is a functioning business. There will come a time when you will look to streamline the process of getting from lab to commercial product, but you will start with a realistic view of what is needed.

Now some of the potential investors to whom you present this plan will say, 'Three and a half years is way too long. Do it in two years and we will back you,' because they have no idea what the challenge is that is ahead of you. To succeed, you must avoid these investors and find others who are more sophisticated. It may be that one of the large contract engineering firms that you hope will eventually build a full-scale plant, or a contract manufacturer will see the potential in what you are proposing and become a cornerstone investor in your business. This is a great validation of both the original idea and the way you have set about implementing it and will persuade others to invest in you. Moreover, their input, at every step, will reduce the risk of failure. Effectively, they will increase both the quantity and quality of your engineering team.

For large swathes of the technology start-up world, getting the right engineering team in place is the most critical factor in success. It is not that hard to do. Getting it right first time requires a mindset and an understanding of the critical engineering problems that any technology company faces on the road from idea to product. If you once have that mindset, being in a location where there is a good supply of engineering talent makes it easier to build your team. Company leadership, both executives and board members, need to recognize the importance of this right at the outset and act upon it with conviction.

Which brings us neatly to the question of leadership: founders, executives, and board members. It is certainly not automatic, indeed it is unusual, for founders of technology start-ups to have what it takes to lead a company from its birth to being a functioning business. Leadership can be developed, but someone must be willing to invest in that development, and the founders need to be sufficiently self-aware that they know what they don't know. How does leadership, or the lack of it, become a cause of start-up failure?

REMEMBER THIS TO IMPROVE YOUR CHANCE OF SUCCESS

➢ Going from lab or basement to a big business is about engineering; recognize this from the outset, plan for it and hire accordingly. Quality is more important than quantity, but you will need both. Hire for quality, contract for quantity.

➢ Engineering is many disciplines, and you will need more of them than you can afford to hire. Contract engineering firms are important partners; get the best you can attract and afford, not the cheapest.

➢ Location in a technological cluster makes it easier to find and hire good engineers.

➢ Customers have high expectations of reliability. Never sacrifice this for lower cost.

➢ The leadership team must have at least one person steeped in engineering. The most crucial thing they need to tell founders and investors is whether you can ever make and sell this product at a cost that will enable you to make money.

Notes

1. Ken Makovsky, 'The Reason CEOs Fail: An Update', *Forbes*, 22 July 2012, www.forbes.com/sites/kenmakovsky/2012/03/22/the-reason-ceos-fail-an-update/, accessed 15 February 2025.
2. John Doerr, *Measure What Matters: How Google, Bono, and the Gates Foundation Rock the World with OKRs* (London: Portfolio/Penguin, 2018).
3. Michael Porter, *The Competitive Advantage of Nations*, 2nd edn (New York, NY: Palgrave Macmillan, 1998).

6

The Fourth Cause of Failure

Leadership

The technology has to work. It has to be able to work at scale, produced at a cost and sold at a price that will eventually allow us to make money. The market must be there, or able to be created and accessed. Moreover, we have to understand the market well enough to know how to sell our offering. Start-ups may begin with one or two people running on a shoestring budget, but if they are going to be real businesses they quickly become larger, requiring more people. The founders have to make the tough transition from scientists and inventors to leaders.

Great companies are built and prosper when they have great leaders. Sometimes, often in the first stages of their life, they stumble along with average or, more often, untrained leaders. Nonetheless, over many decades, experience says that a lack of high-quality leadership is a great predictor of failure. Venture investors will often tell you that they back the CEO, that it is probably 50 per cent or more of their decision of whether to invest. If I was being a bit cynical, I would say that they make the CEO such a high percentage of the decision because they think they can evaluate the CEO and their chance of success, whereas they can barely figure out what the technology is about. And yet, six months, a year or two years later they are disillusioned with the very leader in whom they were so enthusiastic to invest. If only they could recognize the type of problem they were taking on with the new leader; if only they could discern that this person was not a leader at all. What are the types of CEOs who are destined to fail their investors?

I spoke at a dinner for investors and CEOs of a venture fund not long ago, and talked about the diverse types of CEOs who were causes of failure in their companies. Afterwards, several of them came up to me to ask, 'Which type of bad CEO do you think I am?' Well, there is a lesson here about the importance of self-awareness as a starting point for improvement, and we are not just talking about incremental improvement. If you are weak, you better become good, and if you are good you need to become great. The challenge is that this growth needs to occur while you are doing all the other hard things involved in building a business.

If there are some distinct types of CEOs whose faults lead to a higher risk of failure, the first job is to recognize the problem when we see it. Let's look at the problem children.

Founders as Chief Executives: A Typology of Bad

Company founders can be individuals with an idea whose time they believe has definitely come; professors who have made a discovery in the lab that will be a business and not just another paper in a good journal; graduate students of some of those very same professors who see business potential in their research and want to exploit that potential rather than have academic careers like their mentors; or serial inventors. Yet another route is founders who are working in a company, have some ideas in the same or a related industry, and would rather work for themselves than make their boss or shareholders rich. Perhaps the company even encourages them to leave and take their ideas with them. There are some people who seem to be natural inventors, and have been among the most successful entrepreneurs – Thomas Edison being the great example who made wide ranging inventions leading to big businesses in electrical devices and the provision of electricity, and also founded leading companies in fluoroscopy, rubber manufacture, chemical synthesis, mining and cement manufacture. In a society that favours and promotes entrepreneurship (and there are great differences in the climate for entrepreneurship between countries,[1] even regions within the same country) founders come in all shapes and sizes.

Wherever they come from, the founder of a company usually starts by seeing themselves as the chief executive, the CEO, of the company they are founding. Sometimes it is two people (Bill Gates and Paul Allen, for example) and they sort out roles between themselves – I will be CEO and you will be CTO, as a frequent solution, or in the case of Gates and Allen, one becomes President and Chairman, the other Vice Chairman. I will return the problems that can occur when there are two founders who have some sort of relationship – spouse, lover, long-term friendship.

Start-ups fail when the CEO is definitely the wrong person, and I want to unpack what 'wrong' means. This can be a founder who has the wrong mindset, is lacking in necessary competencies, is missing key skills (the distinction between skills and competencies is important here, and I will discuss it further at the end of this chapter), and perhaps most important, doesn't have the self-awareness to know that they have a problem or that they are the problem.

The Tech Person as CEO

The first type of these CEO founders is the most innocent: The Purely Technical Leader. This person sees the opportunity, the competitive advantage, guesses how big the market could be, they have the vision for the business. They have nothing else that is needed for leadership. They have never hired people for a variety of posts, led a team of people to achieve a goal or perhaps they have been supervising doctoral students for several years and think that the team in the business will be like that. It isn't. The ability to build an effective team is the central competency that any business leader needs to have.

As regards doing business, this technical founder usually thinks it is pretty simple: there is income, there is expenditure. When income is more than expenditure, the company is making a profit, which is a good thing. Is there anything else I need to know? In other words, they have no conception of working capital, cash management, the role of debt, depreciation and other non-cash items, what is a balance sheet and how to read one – need I go on? Basic financial skills are lacking, and there is no awareness on the part of the leader that having these skills is important to the success of the company.

Now all of these things about business are pretty easy to learn, the founder just has to appreciate their importance and decide to get educated. It is a lot easier to learn the fundamentals of business accounting, essentially a set of skills, than it is to hone your abilities at hiring, leading, and shaping a team to do a hard job solving difficult problems, which is a core competency. You must still master both the basic business skills and the leadership competencies. In my experience, building the team-leadership competency usually requires a willingness to engage in significant personal development with the help of a coach or mentor. Suppose that the technical founder has no interest in getting the business skills or the leadership competencies required to lead the company? One way out of the problem is to decide that the founder is not the business leader but the technical leader of the company. I will return to the question of whether the purely technical founder is best suited to the role of CTO.

Money Raising Person as CEO

The second type of failure-prone founder is one of the most dangerous: The Great Fundraiser. These founders know just what buttons to press to convince venture capital partners or angel investors to part with their money, often copious quantities of it. How often have I heard partners in a venture capital firm remark, after hearing a pitch from one of these founders, 'Well, I'm not sure about the business, but that guy is definitely backable.'

This should be fine, if the business proposition is sound and the founder knows what he needs to make it a reality instead of an idea. The problem is that this great salesperson founder is so taken up with selling the remarkable story that they don't see the numerous challenges that lie ahead. When any of these are raised – 'You said the eventual cost per device will be 15 per cent of what it is today, tell me how will you get the cost of the units down?' 'Where will the products be manufactured?' 'How will you access the Asian market which you say is crucial to success?' – the salesperson founder has stock answers to brush these aside: 'The costs come down as volume increases'; 'We plan to outsource the manufacturing to a great contract manufacturing firm in Noplace, Idaho'; 'We have already set up a relationship with a group in Vietnam to take us into Asia' (that is, I called my friend's college roommate whose girlfriend is Vietnamese). Recalling failure cause 3, this founder does not see the need for a strong engineering team to solve problems that will occur between idea and reality, because he doesn't believe that such problems could actually exist.

Most Arrogant Person as CEO

A third type of high failure rate founder is: The Arrogant. Now a certain amount of arrogance is necessary, perhaps even desirable, in someone who is pushing the boundaries and disrupting an industry. When the founder believes that they are much smarter than they actually are, they will not take advice from the board or others, inside or outside the company. Indeed, they will react to proffered advice in a way that discourages people from giving it again. Charlie Munger once said he would rather work with a CEO who had an IQ of 130 but believed it was 120, than one who had an IQ of 140 and believed it was 170.

The problem with arrogant founders is that they are so confident, so sure of themselves, that they trivialize the importance of everyone else's job. Problems with valves clogging? Engineering will sort that out. Patents being challenged? That's what I pay lawyers for. You would think that venture investors, having seen this sort of founder before, would be loath to back such a person, knowing that disaster will follow. Quite the opposite. Too often the venture investors see in the arrogant founder just the sort of qualities they admire, and which they show in their own behaviours. Arrogance that is not justified by their abilities or insight.

Media Star CEO

The fourth type of founder who often fails is: The Media Star. Inevitably, the more appealing the start-up idea, the more disruptive it is, the greater the attention it receives from press, television, TED talks and online media. There is a demand for the CEO to appear and talk about the company and how it is going to upend the entire world of (you fill in the blank). Now most founders demur from this or maybe do one or two interviews, knowing that they have more important work to do if the company is going to succeed. However, there is a subset of CEOs who find that they love the attention, and moreover they are good at it. When it comes to discussing the company, and its mission, they are articulate and convincing, able to intersperse humour with some light technical explanation. As a result, they get more invitations, which they accept. Sure, this is taking away time from running the company but, they rationalize, it is building momentum for the idea, undoubtedly increasing the company's valuation. Moreover, it is something I can do, while there are other people back at the company who are able to solve the day-to-day problems with the business. While he would probably see it differently, I would argue that Shai Agassi of Better Place was in this category of media star CEO, who had the ability to lead the company to a more successful outcome but spent too much doing public events.

This is the opposite of leadership. It is effectively absenting yourself from the job to do something you enjoy more. In moderation it is fine, of course it is. When it becomes 20, 30, 100 interviews it is not fine. It says something about the company's leadership to which the investors better pay attention. However, they often don't pay attention to it, because they are focused on increasing the company's paper valuation, rather than building a substantive, well-led business. All these media interviews may be supporting a hyped-up valuation; however, they are not contributing to building a company with sound foundations.

These are four types of CEO leadership failures that occur over and over again. When companies make it through the first few years of life, they have technology that works and are beginning to get some traction in the market, it is failure of leadership from one of these types that often takes the company down.

Lead Me Not into Temptation

Sadly, there are other problems with company leadership than the four types just described. One of these relates to having too much money in too immature or immoral hands.

When a company is funded with a substantial round, the CEO finds him or herself able to make decisions on spending large amounts of money, compared to what they may have been used to as a student, young worker, or even as an employee of a corporation from which they have spun out a venture. Most people are honest and have a keen sense of accountability to their shareholders and to their fellow employees/partners on how that money is spent. Occasionally, this is not the case.

I was on the board of a start-up where the CEO decided that the company needed some new brochures and promotional materials. Although his daughter lived on another continent and had no familiarity with the company or its activities, he awarded her a significant contract to design these materials. This is not stealing the money, though it is close, and it occurs more often than we would like to believe.

Another CEO felt that the company should be paying for his health insurance. Nothing wrong with that, although they did not pay health insurance for any of the other twenty-four employees. He could have asked the compensation committee of the board for this benefit, and they might have agreed or turned him down. He didn't do this. He simply took company funds and bought himself a health insurance policy.

You might ask, what was the Chief Financial Officer (CFO) of any of these companies doing while all this was happening? The answer is simple: In every case the CEO felt that there was no need to have a CFO at this early stage of a company; it would be sufficient to have an accountancy firm that put together the numbers after the fact. Indeed, it was only when one of these accountancy firms contacted me as Board Chair and said, 'This may be ok, I just want to know if you agreed to it?' that the problem became known.

There are cases where the CEO transfers investor funds into a personal bank account. These are thankfully pretty rare, though not unknown. They are most likely to occur when the whole business is a complete fraud, so we already know that the founder has no moral scruples. Nonetheless, the more subtle misuses of investor funds are something that do occur. By siphoning off funds that are needed to make the company a success, they increase the risk of failure.

'Lifestyle' Companies

It doesn't happen often, but there are some people who so enjoy running their little companies that they really don't want them to get any bigger, or for anything to happen that will disrupt the pleasure they get from being in charge. On the other hand, they would like your money to fund their lifestyle.

Some years ago, my partners and I were looking for companies with innovative technologies in a particular area relating to water. Experts pointed us to a small company in the UK, which seemed to have something interesting and original, possibly disruptive. They were not raising money; indeed, the company was already listed on a special part of the London Stock Exchange for newer, small companies. We thought that was not a problem, we could persuade them that they would be better off as a private company, with us able to inject substantially more funds than they could raise in the public markets.

So off we went to see the two leaders of the company, in a small office in London's suburbs. Everything about the company checked out. They did indeed have something innovative, they had already built the first small plant, and there was interest in perhaps a second plant in the Middle East. And no, they were not particularly interested in our offer.

Why? Because they knew that if we came on board, we would be trying hard to supercharge the company, especially given that they had a competitor in the US who was a bit behind them doing something similar. These two middle-aged gentlemen, who had had moderately successful business careers, were quite happy coming to the office three days a week, managing a couple of staff, taking small salaries and toddling along at their own pace. It suited their lifestyle. Well, at least they were completely honest in not wanting our money, or our advice.

This is a particular type of start-up leadership that leads to eventual failure (and the company is now gone, the two gentlemen happily retired I guess) because you cannot revolutionize an industry by sitting in an office, drinking coffee in the morning and gin and tonics in the afternoon three days a week. Most venture capitalists will avoid lifestyle companies because of the ambition mismatch between the company leaders and the venture capital partners.

Are You Committed?

Promising ideas for new companies often come out of academic labs these days. Professors, and the universities that employ them, have seen business opportunities emerging from their research work for a long time. In the past this mostly led to patents that the university licenced to others to commercialize, usually with little reward, occasionally producing a lot of wealth for the university, for example with the University of Wisconsin patents on Warfarin, or many seed patents that resulted from agricultural research at US universities. Increasingly over the last fifty years there are a stream of companies being formed by faculty members and their students. Perhaps the most prolific of such professors is Robert Langer of MIT, who has been behind the founding of forty companies. Nobel Prize winner Carolyn Bertozzi of Stanford has also founded many companies.

All of this is fine, appropriate, and an important source of economic activity for any country or region. When common sense prevails, the faculty member does one of two things: Usually, in cooperation with a good venture capital firm, they find a competent CEO to lead the new company, sometimes this is a recent PhD from the group who was involved in the discovery, with the faculty member having both an economic interest in the company and providing ongoing advice and counsel, especially around new scientific/technological developments. Occasionally, a faculty member says, 'this is really important, I am so committed to it that I will leave my faculty post because I want to lead the new company'. Rarely, but sometimes, they have the skills and temperament to do so. A notable example of this was Professor Larry Evans from MIT, whose research group developed the ASPEN software. He left to form Aspentech, and led it for several decades, growing it into a multibillion-dollar business.

So now for the problem case: A faculty member says, 'This company is important, and I am the brains behind it, so I will be the CEO. However, I am not leaving my university post, I will still be doing that as well. After all, I am a tenured professor and have responsibilities to my research group and students. Don't worry, I have plenty of time to lead the company while being a professor.'

This is not a level of commitment that will lead to success. One way or another, disaster is inevitable. The company does not get the attention it needs, or the leadership it requires. Because the professor has added the company to his roles, but not changed his thinking about what is important, business development in the company is neglected in the interest of new science. The university frequently becomes unhappy because the professor is not to be found at regular campus obligations. Sometimes, there is a profound commitment to both jobs, and it is too much for one person to bear.

Every venture investor knows in their heart that a successful start-up needs a CEO with a full-time commitment, with a lot at stake in making the company a success. That is incompatible with simultaneously being a tenured professor. So why do investors sometimes accede to the request/demand by the professor that they be the CEO even without that commitment level? Because they are ignoring yet another reason why start-ups fail.

Companies Grow – Do Their Leaders?

Some years ago, I was on the board of a company that had just received substantial amounts of venture funding from three different firms. The originators of the idea were two recently graduated PhD students, and these young scientists were eventually convinced by the investors to have a CEO, with whom they had no connection at all, brought in from outside. This CEO had a great track record with early stage highly scientific businesses. I was an external director nominated by the two scientists and agreed to by the venture investors.

Now what was remarkable at the time, and still impressive to me, is that when we met this prospective CEO he said something like this:

I am the best CEO you can get for the first two to two and a half years of a company like this. I will do everything in my power to get it up and running quickly as a viable business. I also know how to make the founders work with me effectively, because I have done it before. And you will pay me a salary, of course, though mostly I want my reward to be in equity in the business because I believe that will be worth a lot in the long run. However, [and this is the key point] I will not be *the best* CEO for the next stage, so as we come up to the two-year mark, start looking for my successor, 'cause I'm outta here!

When we consider the top team – CEO, Chief Operating Officer (COO), CFO – of a start-up, and particularly the CEO, there are two important things to realize if your goal is avoiding failure. A workable company, one that is making progress from its founding to being a going concern, is changing rapidly. If it is not changing rapidly, it is probably stagnant which is another way of saying that it is failing. Assuming the company is making progress, the right CEO for the first two years is probably the completely wrong person for the next two, and the ideal candidate for years four to ten might be different again. The second point follows directly from this: very few people in the CEO role will be sufficiently self-aware to know when they are not able to do the job.

But what about . . . you will say, naming two or three counter examples. Of course, the best people grow, learn, adapt their behaviours. They are not exactly exceptions, because growth and development are what we should expect from a leader. It just doesn't happen in every case, probably it doesn't happen in most cases. We humans get into a certain mode of action as leaders. If we are sensitive to the impact of what we do, when something seems to be effective, we do it again, and hopefully we avoid repeating our less effective interventions. We find it difficult to stop doing something that used to be effective when the company was five people but doesn't work at all when there fifty people. Great leadership coaches help CEOs make changes to their behaviours, but start-ups cannot afford them. The most precious thing a start-up leader can have is a respected CEO of another company, perhaps one who is retired, who will help guide and nurture them through multiple periods of change.

The first two to three years of a company bring very particular leadership challenges: building a core team, solving a lot of problems, getting first traction for the product in the market. By contrast, the next period might involve a transition to manufacturing at scale, having a proper sales force rather than going directly to early-stage customers, perhaps negotiating with partners who are channels to the market, contracting with larger engineering firms, relationships with government. Often the transition is from a team where everyone works on several different things, behaves to some extent as generalists even if they have specialist education, to a team with a lot of specialists. Recruiting and managing these two distinct kinds of teams demands different competencies. Making the transition as a leader requires quite a lot of self-awareness, growth, and sophistication.

Because of this transition in company needs, the same behaviours that worked in the early stage don't continue to be effective. The leader must adapt and change to deal with the new things facing her. It is the self-aware CEO in this situation, or even before the first stage has begun to conclude, who foresees that the challenges ahead are not the ones that she enjoys, rather it is the early build stage they love, and tells the board it is time for new leadership.

Sadly, that is rare. The usual mode of behaviour is, 'I'm in charge, I'm doing a good job, and continue backing me as the leader of this enterprise.' Someone must step in, and that is the role of the board, which I will be discussing in more detail in a later chapter.

How do you know when the company has outgrown its leader? The first answer is simply RESULTS. Any well-governed company has a set of targets it is committed to achieving in the coming quarter, six months, and year. The first and most important warning sign of leadership is when the company is not achieving these objectives while it is still burning through its cash at a rapid rate.

The second warning sign is disaffection or loss of key staff. Companies have employee turnover, even when they are start-ups, as good people seek opportunities for themselves. It is not necessarily a terrible thing, though there are often a few people in early-stage companies who are crucial to its success. There are all sorts of reasons why people leave. The board and investors need to be extremely sensitive to any hint that staff departures are because of a lack of confidence in the CEO, or worse, because of what staff see as bad behaviour by the leadership. That is a sign that unless a change is made the probability of failure has increased.

Leadership Brought in From Outside

In earlier venture capital days, it was quite common for investors to explain to founders that the company needed skills, competencies, and experience that they, the founders, did not have. Hence a CEO would be found with just those things, and the investors would convince that person to join and lead the company. In some cases, as I described in the earlier section, which would be a 'first two years' specialist. In my experience, and I have seen this several times, it works well. There is a job to do convincing the founders that this is in their best interest. The best of the venture guys, who are the least arrogant ones, are skilled at doing this. They also know several people who would be good fits for the CEO role.

I think it is unfortunate that this has become less and less common, and it is undoubtedly due to the rise of the superman/superwoman founder, Jeff Bezos, Sergey Brin, Mark Zuckerberg, who succeeded as CEOs and grew their companies from nothing into giants. Increasingly, founders see themselves as being 'one of those guys' and are convinced they can do it too. A few of them can, most of them cannot. With this attitude on the part of founders, it is much harder for investors to convince them to put their precious baby, this start-up, into the leadership hands of someone they don't even know. Understandable? Yes, of course it is. Nonetheless, it could be that the model of external leadership was the winning one and should not be abandoned if we want to reduce failure rates.

An Alternative Role for The Founder

Investors often try to find an alternative role for a company founder, especially when that person is a scientist or engineer rather than a businessperson who wants to be a part of the company on a full-time basis and for the long term. Finding that role makes it easier to implement the entry of external leadership as discussed in the earlier section.

The usual and obvious way through this is that the technically inclined founder becomes the CTO. This is logical, seems to fit the skill set, opens the way for a CEO who can lead and develop the business. So, is it the way to avoid failure?

Yes. And no.

CTO of a technology start-up seems like a pretty important job. When we have an important job, do we fill it by giving it to someone who isn't qualified to do a different important job? It is certainly possible that the technical founder is the person most knowledgeable about the technology and best placed to both solve problems while driving the technology forward. In considering what is meant by 'drive it forward', we must recognize that the first iteration of an innovative technology may be an advance on what has gone before, but it is just that – a first iteration. There need to be many more. When someone says, well we have invented this device/process/app and now we just need to bring it to market, that shows a lack of appreciation of how innovations develop. Swan or Edison's first light bulbs were nothing like the ones being sold ten years later, and have had many successors, the first several of which improved the quality of light, lifetime, and convenience of incandescent bulbs. And then there were fluorescents, neon, halogen and LEDs. We are probably not finished with the evolution of the light bulb. Who drives these successive waves of innovation? The CTOs leading a technology team of the companies that have strong, enlightened leadership.

Too often venture investors, with an eye on a quick and highly profitable exit, which is after all how they are rewarded, see evolving the technology as a waste of both time and money, and a diversion from the goal. Make it work, sell it, build lots and deliver. With this attitude, they believe that the CTO can be someone with an interest in the company as a founder who needs to get out of the way of those leading the business to where it is generating more cash than it is spending. This puts added pressure on the person who is CTO. In deciding that a technical founder should be CTO, we must question whether that person has the vision for the second, third, and later iterations of the product, as well as the ability to convince investors to back that vision.

Lacking a strong CTO, with investors keeping the company focused on selling what we have now, often turns out to be a not particularly clever way for ensuring failure, because it means that a different company, that is able to think and act for the longer term, ultimately gets the big prize. The lesson here is that while the technical founder might be a great person to be CTO, be sure that they have clear objectives that are going to support and enhance value in the future company.

Who Needs a CFO?

I want to return to a point made earlier about avoiding financial irregularities, with a different emphasis, by asserting that when a company gets to a certain key stage in its growth it needs a proper CFO. Furthermore, many times the CEO does not appreciate this, and the board, too focused on controlling costs while driving revenue, does not see the need for it either. Board members might consider themselves to be financial experts (because they don't understand the technology so they must be there for some reason) so believe that they can provide enough of a CFO function without someone being hired for this role.

Earlier in this section I said that this opens the risk of fraud on the part of the CEO, especially when even accounting services are done by an external firm, and the CEO signs off on all purchases and invoices. To deal with that problem, the company doesn't necessarily need a proper CFO, just a good internal controller who has enough independence of the CEO that they can go to the board with any concerns. The CFO role is much greater than this, and in my view is needed earlier in the life of the company than is often assumed.

Here is a suggestion that is somewhat arbitrary, ('rules' in business often are arbitrary). When a company has raised more than £10 million, it needs a CFO. Before this, there is probably not enough certainty or cash available to attract a competent CFO, though there can be exceptions. In the pre £10 million stage, accountancy and control are essential. This is quite distinct from what is meant by the role of a CFO.

At this £10 million+ stage, there are employees, contracts to be entered, banking relationships to be started/built and cash to be managed. Depending on the specifics of the business, there may be significant working capital requirements, which will be discussed further when we consider money or the lack of it as a cause of failure. The board needs to see a quality financial plan for the company. There was probably an aggressive plan for building revenues and getting to the point of positive cash generation laid out in the fundraising pitch. Now what is needed is a financial plan that shows what will happen if those goals are achieved and looks at one or two upside and downside cases. The most important question everyone should be asking, no matter whether we are meeting plan or not meeting plan, is, 'When will we run out of cash?' If the business grows more rapidly than plan, can our supply chain respond, and will we have the working capital to fulfil demand? All these requirements mean that there needs to be a proper CFO in place.

Looking ahead, in almost every case I have seen, a company that has raised £10 million will have to raise more money in the future. If they are successful, it might be significantly more. If the company is making widgets, success may mean considerable needs for working capital, and it would be best if that can be done without giving away more equity. A CFO will be able to deal with banks, government funders of export finance or other government loan funds, existing and new investors, in a way that can give them confidence beyond what the CEO can provide as a vision for the business.

The CEO, unless they have been down this road before, will often not see this need, indeed in some cases will resist it. It is up to the board in most cases to make the CEO recognize that a CFO will allow them to focus on other things, things that they are better equipped to do. A good CFO will also be a sounding board for the CEO, helping them sharpen their ideas and present them better.

Every investor knows that if you want to fail, the easiest way is to not manage cash. Not every venture investor, certainly not every technical founder, sees that there is a lot more to this than just adding up positive and negative numbers each month and hoping that the result is positive. A CFO, at a certain stage of a business' life, can materially reduce the risk of failure.

Leadership: What Type are You? How to Learn and Grow

Leadership development to succeed in a start-up, probably in any business or role we take on in life, begins with awareness. As numerous behavioural psychologists have put it, what is important is awareness of self, awareness of others, and from that comes appreciation of differences. We all struggle with this, because it is about our ultimate maturity, and everyone in a leadership position who has some level of self-awareness will appreciate that they could do with more maturity in how to approach the challenges they face. To make a company successful through leadership development is thus one of the most difficult barriers to overcome.

The role of leadership is to enable success, that is, to make decisions as a result of which others can make the company succeed. To approach this, I want to return to the distinction between skills and competencies, and then talk about how to develop competencies in start-up leadership.[2] To begin an explanation of what are skills and what are competencies, I am going to use a simple example, and then connect it to the start-up world.

We all think we know what skills are. They are, effectively, expert knowledge that a person gets through learning and practice. Suppose a member of staff has been promoted from running a pizza restaurant to a new role opening branches in a pizza chain. This employee requires a certain set of skills to open a new pizza restaurant for the company. He needs to know how to secure the real estate, get the equipment and furniture ordered, hire the key staff, secure the appropriate staff training so it meets the chain's standards, and check on the quality of product and service both in the first week and later after opening.

But does he have the competencies needed to do this new responsible job successfully? Having hired the key staff, can he quickly build them into a team? Is he astute enough to understand the relationships that need to be built with other local merchants? Will he be able to motivate the new store manager to achieve exceptional performance? How does he react to changes in the business environment? And beyond all that, assuming he aspires to a still larger role in the company, does he have the competencies to think through what the future strategy is on opening new stores? If he has ideas about this strategy, will people listen to him? If he is put in charge of a bold new venture, (say, expanding the pizza chain's network to Uzbekistan), will he be able to build the team in this unfamiliar environment to carry it out successfully? Even if he can build that team, will it align behind him or go in several different directions.

Skills and competencies are two quite different things, and it is the astute start-up company leadership, both the executives/founders and the investors/board, that recognizes this and thinks deeply about it. Mostly they think about skills because it is easier. As with everything else in this book, to succeed you must work on the difficult things.

In start-ups, and this is true in all businesses, as a person progresses, of course she develops and expands her skills. She also must recognize the need to develop new competencies. Think of competencies as fitness. Indeed, they are fitness for purpose. Unless we have this fitness, we will not practice our skills effectively. I think this is clear to all of us in the pizza restaurant example: we have probably all seen someone who had mastered every skill required to do a job like this, who still made a total mess of it because they lacked the required competencies. When we see someone with the sorts of competencies I described for the pizza chain, we know we are watching a talented person in action.

A possible set of competencies that I didn't invent but have found useful is shown in the 3 x 3 grid that follows. There is nothing about these that should be viewed as prescriptive. Each company can figure out its own and should do so. Indeed, the process of coming to these involves a lot of interviews with leaders of the Company at several levels, to see what they consider to be important, both to success of the Company, *as well as for an individual* to be successful in the Company, alignment of these two being crucial. Still, that process of teasing out competencies is something of a luxury for an early-stage company, so why not just steal something someone else has already done?

Respected Player	Acts Wisely and Decisively	Leads Change
Strategic Influencer	Builds Best Teams	Shapes Performance
Strategic Conceptualizer	Environmentally Astute	Ensures Alignment

There is a reason 'Builds Best Teams' is at the centre of this grid. If you fail on this, the chances are that the company will fail. There is no single way to build an effective team. We see in the sports world that coaches and managers can be successful or not with quite different approaches.

Surrounding the centrality of team building, I would suggest that, for senior leadership, core competencies must include something about strategic ability, hence the competencies of Strategic Conceptualizer and Strategic Influencer. The leader needs an awareness of what is going on around you external to the company, which is what I mean by Environmentally Astute, and when they speak internally or in the community, they are listened to, so a Respected Player. With all of this there must be a relentless drive to execute, so a person who Ensures Alignment behind goals, Leads Change rather than being stuck with one way of doing things, Shapes Performance and is perceived by all to Act Wisely and Decisively. Core competencies for leadership are about strategic thinking, ability to influence others both within the company and externally, as well as a relentless drive to deliver on commitments.

It is easy to teach skills and to evaluate how well these skills have been learned. It is much harder to develop competencies and to evaluate how well these are practiced. Some leaders seem to work on the assumption that skills are taught but you must be born competent – 'either you got what it takes or you don't'. I disagree. I know that my own competencies have developed a lot over my management career, some through courses I have taken, a lot through being observant of the leaders I have worked with, still more through receiving feedback and acting on that feedback. Competency development for an up-and-coming staff member is why we think carefully about the assignments they are given, and with whom they will be working on these assignments. For the leaders of a start-up, it is a clear responsibility of the board, particularly the chair, to help the CEO, CTO and CFO, Sales/Marketing leader, develop the competencies they need to make the company a success.

It's obvious that not everyone can be raised to the highest level of skills in a particular area – again, we know this from the sports world. Nor can everyone be developed to the highest level of competency needed to lead a company. If the leaders of the company are sufficiently self-aware to appreciate where they lack competencies, and take steps to fill these gaps, sometimes they emerge as able to go beyond perceived limits. When they don't, it becomes important for the board to act to remedy the deficiencies.

I started this chapter by describing several types of leaders who can cause a company to fail. What I am asking every start-up leader to do is honestly assess themselves in terms of these types and decide to get better at what they do. If you are missing certain skills, for example if you are a technical founder who needs to learn some basic business principles, figure out how you are going to remedy these deficiencies and act on it. More likely, if you can recognize that there are competencies that you need that you have never developed, think about who is going to coach you on these – hopefully someone on your board, or the leader of a company who you know, admire and trust.

If you are a member of the board of a start-up, what are you doing to develop the competencies of the company's leadership? I would suggest that in the weeks or months after an initial funding round, when the board is having its first meetings, one thing it needs to do is assess the competencies of the key individuals, decide where there are weaknesses (because there certainly are some), and assign responsibility for trying to improve. Then, periodically, assess whether progress is being made. If it is not, ask what we are going to do differently.

Great leadership is so important to success, yet it is often assumed that when it is not working the only solution is to replace the leader with a new one. That may be the right answer, though likely it is the higher risk approach to solving the problem. Remedying skills deficiencies promptly and building leadership competencies gradually are two of the most important things we can do to ensure start-up success.

Throughout this discussion of leadership, we have seen examples where the board needs to guide, support, mentor, evaluate, and sometimes change the management. By playing this and other roles, great boards can enable the success of the company. Do the job badly, and the board can be a cause of failure. It is that cause that we explore in the next chapter.

REMEMBER THIS TO IMPROVE YOUR CHANCE OF SUCCESS

- ➤ There are a set of skills that leaders need to have. Assess where the gaps are in your training and experience, and get help to learn these skills. Scientific founders may be particularly weak in financial skills, and need to learn these.

- ➤ Competencies are different from skills, and yet are crucial for building and leading great teams. Do a self-assessment and ask your top team for their views. If you can afford it, get a professional coach. Or ensure that your board Chair is a person who can help you develop competencies you are missing.

- ➤ Start-ups, if they survive the early stages, have different leadership needs as they grow. The right leader for the early stage may not be the best person for a growth phase. Be self-aware enough to know whether you can make that transition.

- ➤ The CTO is a key position for a technology start-up. It is not a job for an unsuccessful founder.

- ➤ As soon as a company can afford a CFO, they should get one. This is a job that goes well beyond accountancy; it can be a key factor in raising and managing large sums of money crucial for growth.

Notes

1   Global Entrepreneurship and Development Index (GEDI), Entrepreneurship & Business Statistics | GEDI, https://thegedi.org/global-entrepreneurship-and-development-index/, accessed 24 May 2025.

2   This section, and many other aspects of leadership in companies that apply to both start-ups and mature companies, were dealt with in my earlier book, *Crash Course: One Year to Become a Great Leader of a Great Company* (London: Whitefox, 2015).

7

The Fifth Cause of Failure
The Board

When angel groups or venture firms invest in a start-up, one of the things included in the negotiations is seats on the company board. Everyone seems to want a voice at the board, and if not full membership then an 'observer' seat. For angel investors, demanding a board seat is often about feeling that is the only way that they can know what is happening, though I have seen angel investors who, as board members or observers, make a huge contribution to early stage start-up companies. I have also seen board observers, and some board members, who are a complete waste of time and space.

With venture firms, the rationale is simple: Their pitch to the founders is, 'We have experience building successful businesses from start-up companies, and as board members we can support you, the entrepreneur, helping you be successful as well.' At the same time, the venture firm has certain interests beyond protecting and nurturing the money it has invested. It is thinking, usually from the outset, about 'how and when I am going to exit this investment (that I just went into) profitably. By sitting at the board, I can ensure that the other investors are also thinking this way and acting accordingly.'

In this chapter, I will explore how the actions and dynamics of a start-up company board can be a cause of failure. The board members, one would think, are completely committed to making the company a success. Nonetheless, by their actions, or sometimes by inaction, they can undermine their own interests.

The Company Leadership and the Board

That companies need to have a board of directors is well established in our capitalist model. Whether it is privately funded companies such as the ones we are dealing with in this book, or those that are trading on the public markets, there is a consensus that a creative tension between management and an independent group of wise and experienced individuals, collectively forming a board, is a necessity.

To consider the role of the board in start-up success or failure, let's divide founders into two groups: Those who are doing this for the first time, and those who have been involved in more than one start-up. The first group is probably a bit naive about the board of the company, its purpose, who they want to have on it, who they are going to have on it whether they want them or not, and even what will happen at board meetings. Gradually, as the legal process of getting the funding progresses (which is their primary focus, since no money, no nothing) the structure of a board emerges.

In the second group, those who have been there before, they are very conscious that a part of what they are going to give up for the money is the control that comes with having a board of directors. They will try to do what is possible to secure a number of seats on the board for themselves, and to limit the number of seats the investors have, although they know that they have limited power to do this. Nonetheless, while the first group may feel that the board is there to help them grow the company, and these are experienced people who know things we don't know, the second group is often more cynical, viewing the board as a necessary evil that they have to accept. This is not always the case; some experienced founders have had a good board experience in a previous venture and know that great board members can help them in innumerable important ways. Still, they also know that it is not a given that the seats on the board will be taken by 'great board members'.

What is usually common to these two groups is a lack of understanding of the role and importance of governance in a company, because governance is what the board does. Governance in a start-up is much different from in a mature public company, nonetheless, there should still be a line between management, what the executives do, and governance, what the board does. Governance, even at the initial stages of a company's life, is important.

The board implements a structured governance of the company, but its primary concerns are strategy and risk. It should be spending a lot of its time on these two areas. At the same time, it is ensuring ethical behaviours, the compensation of leadership (both the principles behind the compensation and the reward itself), compliance with company law and financial regulation, things like that. In a start-up, the board Chair should be a mentor to the CEO, and if there is a CFO, the board member chairing the Audit Committee will be a mentor and confidante of that person. Usually most if not all the board members other than those from management are also there looking out for the interests of a specific investor or group of investors.

These are important roles for a board, and they are distinct from the role of management. **The attitude of the founders/management of a start-up should be that they want to have a better board than they deserve for a company of their age and size.** They should want directors with diverse backgrounds and experience, who will commit themselves to the success of the company. Sadly, they don't always want this, and even when they do, they don't always get it.

What's The Rush on Governance?

One of the ways that boards fail their start-ups is by waiting too long to install proper governance. The board members are completely focused on moving the business forward, keeping the pressure on the CEO and senior leadership, that they don't do their governance job, at least the operational part of it. I have seen too many companies go on for several years without the board putting in place an audit committee, a compensation/remuneration committee, or some basic policies. The board must also agree with management the delegations of authority, at a detailed level. All of this doesn't need to be overly burdensome on either board members or management. It just needs to be there and be functional.

You might think that while this is desirable, it is not a cause of failure. I have already discussed fraud, and I also discussed dishonesty on the part of the CEO, where I raised the lack of proper board oversight on financial matters. Fraud is not just in the technology; it can occur as the company makes its numbers seem better than they actually are. A report by CB Insights found that a significant percentage of start-ups fail due to fraud or mismanagement.[1] According to the report, 23 per cent of start-up failures are due to 'dishonesty' on the part of the company's founders or employees. This can include everything from misrepresenting the company's financials to outright embezzlement.

There is also internal 'dishonesty' that is a cause of failure, if the board does not exercise appropriate oversight. The company prepares a budget, but halfway through the year they are hopelessly behind. So they do a new budget, and then report to the board that they are meeting the revised budget.

Governance mechanisms are there to make sure this doesn't happen. When board members sign off on the company's accounts, governance ensures they have done the work to be confident in the numbers. This work needs to be carried out by a qualified board member, with sufficient financial literacy to interact with the CFO on the one side and the auditors on the other. Even in a start-up, the board composition must take account of this need.

Regarding compensation, investors usually create a pool of stock options that can be granted to employees. The CEO recommends these, while it is the board that grants them. The board must have appropriate leadership *and* mechanisms to agree objectives and determine the levels of share options as well as salaries and bonuses. It seems obvious that this is so important to founder and staff recruitment, motivation, and retention that the board would put in place proper governance processes regarding stock options right from the outset. It doesn't always happen. I have seen it done many times in an ad hoc fashion, sometimes as a negotiation over a beer between the CEO and lead investor. This is poor practice, with the consequences often appearing much later. Incidentally, board members are often compensated through stock options or share grants. This also requires proper governance practice that can be defended to all investors.

Governance, in the form of board committees, policies committed to writing, and following those policies in practice, is not something to 'get to later when the company has grown'; rather it is the right thing to do when the start-up is starting up. In a way, this is the easy part of the process that can avoid failure. Governance, as I have said, is also about the board's time spent on strategy and risk. This is the more difficult part, because it involves thinking, spending intensive time, realism rather than self-deception. It is also the place where management, in their role as members of the board, must step out of their roles as CEO or CFO and behave as board members.

How Boards Fail on Risk

Business is about taking risks, because if you don't take risks, you can never grow the business or distinguish yourself from your competitors. While for an established company risks may be contained and well defined, start-ups seem like they are all risk. Still, the board including the executives and the independent directors must work on this. How does the leadership of the company, executive and non-executive, manage those risks to the best advantage of shareholders?

The evidence for ineffectual risk management in companies is all around us. Even if we set aside large financial institutions, where the examples of poor risk management have dominated the world economy for much of the past decade, the record is poor. Examples are mergers and acquisitions where enthusiasm for the deal overwhelmed the results of due diligence, expansion into new geographies followed by retrenchment from those ventures with great loss of shareholder value, operations which had disastrous safety or environmental performance, inattention to changing regulatory or political climates . . . need I go on? I suspect that you can think of recent examples in each of these categories, and if you can't, you probably have not been reading the business pages of a newspaper recently.

In mature companies, the board has regular agenda items on risk. In start-ups there may be discussion of an explicit risk that is the latest problem, but too often there is not more comprehensive board discussion. Still, even when boards of start-ups decide to devote time to discussing risk, there can be problems.

Even if there is process, and content, to the risk agenda item, it can fail to deliver the guidance that is necessary. From the examples of failure cited above, you can see that while there are always financial consequences, the problems are not usually of the more conventional financial nature – for example, fraud, poor counterparty management, bad debts, cybersecurity and so on. Assuming there is an audit committee, every Audit Committee Chair and most Audit Committee members know how to probe the processes behind managing those sorts of risks. We have become good at that. The problems come from everything else – business strategic decisions, operations, and management awareness of what is going on in the outside world – in other words, from lack of competencies as we have discussed in the previous chapter.

How do we fail in content and process of the risk agenda item?

By focusing on the wrong things entirely: Major risks to the corporation are sometimes cited as, 'We fail to deliver the growth we have promised' or 'We overspend the capital budget.' These are just the basic jobs of management, and citing these as the major risks, usually accompanied by mitigations like, 'Sales force is strengthened to deliver growth' and 'Project managers are held to account for capital budgets on their projects at every stage' just says we will mitigate by doing our jobs properly. No, you cannot take the basic tasks of management and call them the risks. A good test is this: Suppose someone wrote down that the risk is 'we fail to respond to customer inquiries in a timely fashion' and the mitigation was 'we read all emails and open all letters on the day they are received'. If you saw this as a board member you would laugh. Now ask yourself, 'How different are the risks I am being shown from an example like this one?'

Not paying attention to past performance as a guide to future risk: While past performance won't show you everything, you ignore it at your peril. This is difficult in start-ups because there isn't much past performance. However, from the time of investment, the management has made promises, and either they have delivered on these promises or they haven't. When it is the latter, the light that is flashing RISK is that the next promises also won't be delivered. We must understand why and how we are going to mitigate that.

Substituting slick process for substantive presentation: There are any number of beautiful graphics programs available to management for the risk discussion. The board members get their papers, and there is a big foldout chart in many colours displaying the risks. There are axes of frequency and magnitude (the right thing to look at, by the way), coloured blobs whose size indicates the scale of the business, different coloured rings indicating the business unit – you get the idea. This chart is a thing of beauty. I would ask, is it useful as a starter for discussion? It can be, of course. But is a board member likely to take out this chart at the meeting and say, 'Let's look at Risk 16, that the decision of our major customer to place their orders is delayed because they want additional features we have not yet incorporated,' asking the leadership to explain what leads this to happen, how technology can mitigate it, are we developing the technological fix, and if not why not?' Or, Risk 2, that there is a problem with the subsidies for our business in southern Europe, asking 'can you give me your views on how the elections next year in Spain, Portugal and Greece will affect this?' In my experience that is not what happens. The beautiful multicoloured chart comes out, resulting in board members being lulled into thinking that everything is under control. It isn't. The thing that is under control is use of the graphics program.

Spending Time on Too Many Different Risks Rather than Focusing

When a board is given a chart with twenty-five different risks laid out in living colour, there is no prioritization to the risk discussion. In some cases, board members prioritize by going to the upper right-hand corner of the chart, presuming that is where the big, high-frequency risks, are being shown, and concentrate on those. Maybe, though perhaps more discussion of other parts of the chart would indicate that the blob representing Risk 15 is in the wrong place. Wouldn't it be better to pick out three or four things, understand them more deeply, have an in-depth discussion and arrive at actions that need to be taken and reported back to the board?

Not Devoting Enough Time to Special Events

Geographic expansion, acquisitions, a bigger capital project than you have ever done before – for things of this sort the board needs more than just a project presentation where the last slide is about risks. The board would be better off assuming that management has understood the business opportunity, evaluated it carefully, and now the reason for bringing this to the board at all is to have a discussion of the risks. That is the place where the board has the biggest chance of adding value.

The Board Doesn't See the Horse Coming Up on the Outside

Fast growing competitors are the biggest risk to some businesses. Slow but powerful competitors with extensive resources, both people and cash, can be even more of a threat. Innovative technologies making your current main product obsolete are yet another. Management worries about such things, or someone in the company warns about them, but they are not brought to the board for fear that the discussion will not be controllable. The real risks are thus hidden away. The board and management need to develop an atmosphere of trust that encourages difficult issues to be brought up for board discussion.

Independent Directors

As I have already made clear, most or all the board of a start-up consists of founders and investor representatives. If an outside CEO has been brought in to lead, of course that person must be a board member. Sometimes the CFO should be on the board. When looking through the boards of start-up companies, you will often find some other names that have no obvious connection either to the founder or the investors.

Who are these board members? Well, sometimes they are there for a particularly good reason. A company is trying to break into an online retail business, and finds a person willing to join the board with a lot of experience in this domain, who is willing to give guidance and help to the founders, avoiding some pitfalls of which they might not be aware. Having such a person on the board can help improve the chance of success.

What does not necessarily add to success is board members who are there because they are well-known names. Over the last decade I have seen that there are several famous people, usually former political leaders, cabinet secretaries, retired generals, that sort of person, whose names appear on the boards of technology companies. In most cases they have no board experience, no technology experience, often no business knowledge. They are there because their name will be recognizable to funders, regulators, possibly to customers. An extreme case was that of Theranos, where the board included two former US secretaries of state, a retired general and retired admiral, two former US senators, and two former CEOs of companies that had little or no technology component. And this was a company about advancing blood tests.

These board members who are there just 'for show' do not contribute to success and may contribute to failure. The company is not their priority, rather it is whether they believe that the company can add to their personal wealth. They want salaries or at least a generous allotment of shares. Their schedules are often complicated and so board meetings wind up being scheduled for their convenience rather than to meet company needs. When a problem arises, they don't respond quickly. If they would just sit there quietly that would usually be of more value than if they feel the need to speak up during board meetings.

I think I am being pretty clear in my view that putting someone on a start-up board just because they are a famous person, even though they have nothing else to offer the company, is a mistake, detracts from the value of the board and should not be done.

Investor Directors: The First Problem

A start-up is about building a business, usually from no customers, no revenue, no product produced at scale that works reliably and trying to achieve all of the above. It would seem obvious that the board members representing the investors should have competencies that can support and guide the company in at least some of these areas.

Most of the start-ups that are of interest to venture investors have some element of technology associated with them. They may be lightly technical, such as support services for climate impact measurement; moderately technical, for example a company that converts pedal bicycles to electric; or deep tech, whether that is complex software for machine learning/AI, hardware involving photonics and laser physics, or RNA-based vaccines.

Across this spectrum of technological complexity, do the investor directors understand the technology of the business where they serve on the board? Of course, they don't have to be PhD laser physicists, though unless a director has some technical education, they won't be able to understand the potential and the limitations of the business.

A board needs a range and balance of expertise, so I am certainly not saying that all the independent directors need to be scientists and engineers. I do feel that a good minimum test is that even a non-technical person serving on a board should be able to give a coherent explanation of what the company does, how it does that, and why that is advantaged over other ways of tackling the same problem.

How does the lack of technical education/expertise of investor directors manifest itself as a problem? I think it is primarily in not having the right conversations about risk. I have already made clear that one of the key roles of the board is discussing, understanding, and taking a critical view of risks facing the company. If the directors are not capable of understanding the company's technology, they will gravitate towards discussing risks that are not related to it, in areas where they are more confident. That should never be the way one determines how a board risk discussion agenda is determined, but it too often is.

There are secondary ways in which the problem of technically ignorant directors hurts performance. If there is one director with some technical expertise, and the others don't have it, they will inevitably defer to that person. That is not how a board should work. Boards work best when everyone brings their own expertise, and can contribute to technical, financial, and governance matters. When the company is a technology-based start-up, a strong technical presence on the board is essential. Just as it requires effort for the technical person on the board to learn how to contribute to financial matters, so the financial director must do the work to be able to add value to a discussion on technology.

The compounding factor here is arrogance. Venture capitalists, particularly the Silicon Valley version, are arrogant. That is a generalization though in my experience not far off a universal trait. When arrogant people get into a discussion about which they have little competence, they make their points more strongly, rather than just shut up and listen. Either they don't know what they don't know, or they do and are keen to cover it up. In both cases the company is poorly served and may be taken in a bad direction.

If experienced venture capitalists tend to be undeservedly arrogant, completely inexperienced ones tend to be weak and ineffectual. Most venture funds have rapid growth, that is to say, they have no money and then they have several hundred million dollars (pounds/euros) to invest. Or they have raised one fund, got off to a good start, and the climate is right, so they raise another soon thereafter. In both cases, they need to hire people, probably young people who have had one job in, for example, investment banking, and now become part of the firm. Investments are made to deploy the fund capital, and there are a lot of board seats to be filled. Someone has the bright idea that we need to give our young people board experience, so they are appointed to the board of one or two of the new investments.

This can work, or it can be a disaster. It works if you do a lot of coaching and teaching about what a board member does, how to be effective, when to ask for help. It also works if the young inexperienced board member watches the others on the board and sees how they contribute, what are effective and ineffective behaviours, how do we understand risk and performance, what is governance and why it is important. This assumes that there are others who are good role models. If neither of these things are true, no teaching, no role models, then the young investor director ends up doing more to promote the failure of the company than its success.

Investor Directors: The Second Problem

While a board needs to have a diversity of views and expertise, it must be aligned on its objectives for the company, and the time scale over which those objectives will be accomplished. This probably seems simple – everyone invests to make the company a success, grow sales, build margin and so on. So how could the investor directors not be aligned with one another? And with management, who also usually have equity in the company. In practice it is not so simple.

Investor directors are (hopefully) bringing their best competencies to every board. At the same time, they are there to fulfil the agenda of their firm, and more particularly, of the fund which has invested in the company. When these are from pure venture capital firms, as contrasted with corporate venture groups, quasi-state entities, or private investors, the main thing the fund wants to achieve is a highly profitable exit from the company. It is only when there is an exit, either to the public markets (IPO), or via a trade sale that the fund can return money to the limited partners and, after clearing some hurdle, distribute carried interest to the partners in the fund.

So if that is the objective, how does misalignment occur? First, by the exceptions I have noted in the previous paragraph. Companies and venture funds like to get a corporate venture group to invest. If you are an energy start-up and one of the major energy companies takes a share, it is a mark of confidence in the importance of the technology for the market. If you are an AI start-up and one of the FAANG (Facebook, Amazon, Apple, Netflix, Google) companies invests, the value of the company has just gone way up. Venture funds and entrepreneurs love this. In contrast to the normal venture capital fund, the corporate venture group is not measured by the speed or size of an exit. It is probably looking for impact and a broader definition of value. It may be looking further down the road at acquiring the start-up itself. If this is the case, driving valuation upwards is against its interest, while the venture fund has exactly the opposite objective. We cannot imagine a big business where board members have such opposite views of the company's financial goals, but this can occur with start-ups.

There are also various kinds of government entities that have funds to invest in start-ups, and who take board seats. Their objective is different from either the venture fund or the corporate venture group. The government investors, who are often regional in large countries, though national in smaller ones, are driven by economic development: jobs, exports, and how a successful start-up attracts other businesses. They may be satisfied and even proud of a big IPO, much less so by a trade sale that has the potential to take the start-up and move it to another location.

It is certainly possible, indeed common, for investors to have different objectives behind investment in the same company. When these cause the board to not be aligned in how it governs the company, it can be a potent reason for failure. Boards need to sort through these alignment issues up front and check in regularly about them if they are to avoid pulling in conflicting directions.

Greed and Self-Deception

When angels or venture capitalists make an investment, there is a lot of effort behind thinking about what the company could be worth, and when, hence the return they can expect. For very early-stage companies, with angel investors, this is purely speculative, especially as the company may have few if any peers that have exited. With later stage venture investments, especially B, C and so on rounds of investment, money is coming in at a substantial valuation of the company, for example, say, 10 per cent equity at a valuation of $50 million, and two other investors are buying an additional 15 per cent, so that the total new money is $12.5 million, leading to a 'post money valuation' of $62.5 million. Now for the new investors their analysis supporting the investment says that they believe that in three years the company will be worth at least $800 million, but to be conservative they justify the investment on it being worth $700 million, so we will get back more than 10x on our investment.

The company makes progress, not amazing, but progress, and after two and a half years along comes a major player in the field, Hotshot Enterprises, and they offer $400 million for the company. The early investors who came in at extremely low valuations are excited about this, and the employees, who are also shareholders, believe that becoming part of Hotshot will give the company a bright future.

But the later stage co-investors are not so happy. After all, though progress has not been as fast as originally hoped, management has shown them slides confirming their belief that the company was on a strong upward trajectory, and breakthrough to greatness could easily happen in the next 18 months. At which point the company would certainly be worth even more than the $800 million they originally hoped for.

Once again, we have misalignment, this time between those who think the offer is an excellent one, and those who think the company will be worth more than twice as much. Everyone in this business remembers the case of Zuckerberg turning down an offer for Facebook of $1 billion, because he had both the belief and the control to do so, and a year later an investment in the company valued it at $15 billion. But few people remember the hundreds of cases where a company turned down an offer of $400 million and three years later the company was sold for $100,000. There are, sadly, lots of examples of this, and few of the Zuckerberg phenomenon.

In venture investing, as Gordon Gekko said, 'Greed is good,' up to a point, and that point is where it turns into self-deception, or where it crowds out rational analysis.

The Mentoring Role

In any company the Chair of the board must function as a mentor to the Chief Executive. Even when the CEO is experienced and highly competent, the Chair plays a role as sounding board, listener to frustrations, and reactor to ideas that the CEO is considering. More often, in a start-up, the CEO has a few of the skills and competencies required for the job, but there are huge gaps. In this case the Chair's role becomes more crucial.

If the Chair does not exercise this mentoring role, and perform it effectively, he or she is contributing to the failure of the company. There are several reasons why this happens. First, the Chair doesn't understand that this is part of the reason they are there. It is not just to chair board meetings, though they must do that; they are also required to be a mentor to the CEO. If nobody tells you this is part of your job description, and you have not experienced it yourself as a CEO with a mentoring Chair, then it is perhaps understandable that you don't do the job. Then again, if as Chair you don't have the awareness of self and awareness of others that I spoke about in the previous chapter, you might not be particularly good at mentoring. People who have the option often avoid doing things they are not good at.

Second, the CEO may be resistant rather than receptive. Some CEOs that I have worked with will send me materials they have prepared for a presentation and ask for comments, then when I make the comments, they go away, think about it, and come back with a revised version that shows both their understanding of what I have suggested and their own intelligence about what they are trying to convey in the presentation. Others immediately react by telling me why I am wrong. When a Chair tries to perform the mentoring role and is repeatedly rebuffed, it is a natural reaction to stop doing it, or to do less of it. Awareness that this is what is happening means it is probably time to change the CEO.

The third reason is that the Chair is too inexperienced as an executive to be an effective mentor to the CEO. As a result, either they don't try (which shows a certain level of self-awareness) or they do it ineffectively, so that they really don't contribute to the development of the CEO. I have spoken earlier in this chapter about board members from venture firms who have little or no direct business experience themselves, and these directors, when in the role of board Chair, will often be ineffectual as mentors.

Everything just said about the Chair-CEO role applies equally well to the relationship between the Chair of the Audit Committee and the CFO. In a start-up, the CFO might be in his or her first such role, just as the CEO is, and a good audit chair will help them grow from their core competency in accounting and control into being a real CFO for the company, able to think and act strategically.

Too Slow to Make a Change

As a board member, you are sitting in a meeting listening to a back and forth between CEO and board members on results from the previous months, problems in manufacturing, why a key sales person has left, dissatisfaction from a major customer, one of the engineers unhappy with a change in product

– any or all of these things – and the thought goes through your mind, 'this CEO is not up to the job any more. They were fine earlier, but the challenges now are way beyond their level of competence. We're going to have to make a change.' This is all in your mind, not spoken, certainly not at that point. But does this thought lead to action?

In the life of a start-up, six months is a big deal. Lose six months because the company is floundering with poor leadership, and the business might be lost. Lose a year and the probability of failure is way up. Everyone knows this. The board chair and the other board members know this. Despite this, when it comes to action there is a disconnect.

What happens? It is more about what doesn't happen. The thought that this CEO needs to be replaced, and fast, for the good of the company and probably for the good of that individual as well, is not spoken and not acted upon. Maybe it's because everyone is too invested in the individual. Perhaps it was because of them that they invested. Or it was someone that the investors brought in to lead the company, so they are responsible for that person being there, having convinced the technical entrepreneurs that they needed this person to make the company succeed.

Whatever the reason, instead of acting, the board members don't say anything; at most in their private conversations they agree that if things don't get better in the next six months they will have to make a change. If this is compounded by the previous problem I discussed, namely the Chair not being an effective mentor to the CEO, then it is almost guaranteed that nothing is going to improve during this six month period.

Six months later you have a proper mess on your hands, not just a company that is failing to make progress as expected. Of course, it takes time to find a replacement who will be attracted to this mess and want to sort it out. If such a person exists. The board, by not acting on what it knows to be the problem, a problem only it has the power to solve, has contributed to the failure of the company.

The lesson is clear, and it is one that I learned from my colleagues in my first venture capital partner role: The first time you are sitting in a board meeting and thinking, 'this CEO is not going to make it, but this is still a company with great potential', that is the time to get into action to make a change.

Eliminating the Board as a Cause of Failure: Making it the Enabler of Success

Let's start by reiterating my advice at the beginning of this chapter: A start-up should aspire to have a better board than it deserves. If a start-up has some good board members, when there is eventual success the founders can easily recall the critical points at which the board contributed to that success.

What sort of people make good board members? I have observed a lot of them over the years, the good, the bad, and the useless. I have talked a lot in this chapter about the negatives, now let's approach this as a positive. To be a good, even a great board member, a person:

> *Must be interested in the business*: Particularly in the UK, but also in other countries, there are some people who are professional board members. They accumulate a lot of companies and go from one meeting to another, without being specialists in any area or type of company. Some of these people have a lot of wisdom and add value. Unfortunately many people of this type don't really have sufficient curiosity or ability to get to grips with what the business is about, what are the drivers of success, what is distinctive about the product or service, what is the environment in which the company is operating. A good board member must be interested in the business, enough to be able to talk about it with more than a superficial level of understanding, not necessarily at the beginning of their tenure on

the board but certainly six months in. If the subject matter of the company's product is not easily understood, they will get themselves tutored, either by company executives or by other contacts, in this way acquiring the knowledge they need to function as a board member. They don't need to be technical specialists, although a good start-up board will probably include at least one person with deep understanding of the technology.

Wants some ground truth: Any good board member will insist on visiting key operating sites, both at the beginning and regularly during their tenure, talking to employees, possibly to customers, certainly to other shareholders. At least that is always my practice. This means that, coupled with a desire to understand what the business is about, they also want to understand how it is being progressed on the ground. Experienced board members will be able to assess the level of professionalism in the company when they make such visits. They can also judge what sort of company culture exists.

Has a commitment to its success: With the interest in the business comes a passion to see it succeed. Great board members listening to a presentation by management are thinking, how can I help? This is especially true in a start-up, where the management needs more help in making an idea into a business. I love it when a board member is able to say, either at a board meeting or privately to an executive, let's get together in the next couple of weeks and go through that capital programme, or that approach to tax, or that product launch, and the executive knows that this will add value. Great board members and management realize that this is helping, coaching, questioning and challenging; it is not taking over the job of management even a little bit.

Is 'well connected', especially board members for early-stage companies, so able to help: Part of the commitment to success, especially in start-up companies, is that the board members use their network to the company's advantage. They have a vast number of contacts, and they are willing to pick up the phone, or send an email, to connect key management of the company with someone in their network who can help. While I was dismissive of having people on the board because they are famous names or have held high-level positions in government, if these people are willing to use their contacts to further the company's goals that is a way they add value.

Independent of, yet trusted by, management: Now an independent, non-executive board member must really be independent. Hence the rule, in the UK, that nine years is the maximum time on a board as an independent director (besides the independence, more than nine years can get boring!). Management also needs to trust its directors: to be critical, sure, to speak their minds, of course, and never to betray confidences. Board members provide support when it is called for, even in the most difficult of circumstances.

While possibly chosen for a specific expertise, has interests and capability to contribute beyond that, so involved in all aspects of a meeting: Very often when there is a space for a new non-executive director, the board tries to add a person with a particular expertise – someone who knows about regulatory issues, or capital projects, or can really understand what the technical people are talking about. Or maybe it is the new audit chair that is required. No matter what specialist expertise the director brings to the board, they must have interest in making contributions across the full range of matters being discussed. Nothing is a bigger waste of space than a director who only comes to life when his area is being discussed.

Must have a good strategic brain: There are some people who are great at operations, and lousy at strategy. Such people play important roles in companies. I don't think they are of any use at the board table. Yes, board members must be able to contribute to a company's drive for operational excellence, but strategy is crucial to the governance role of the board. In assessing someone's suitability for a board role, better be sure you have determined if the person is able to add value to developing strategy at the highest level.

Doesn't default to second-guessing management: The worst fault in a board member, especially in a chair, comes when they slip into playing management rather than being a good board member. So many board members have been senior executives/CEOs themselves, that they have a lot of ideas on how management should tackle a problem. Contributing those ideas is not their job at the board table. I have seen it happen often, and it is such a waste of everyone's time.

The preceding points are all about the individuals on the board. The most fundamental thing that founders and investors should want from the board as a unit is alignment. The board must all be pulling in the same direction, be agreed on desired pace and outcomes, with all this being in sync with what management has agreed as its performance commitment. Just as I have shown 'ensures alignment' as a leadership competency for the management of the company, so it is a core competency of the Board Chair to ensure alignment. At the first sign that this is not the case, it is the obligation of the board members to pause and do a course correction, because that is the only way to keep the company on the path to success.

Board alignment is important at all stages of the company. We know it can be most difficult when the board and management must deal with opportunities for sale or other exit for the investors. The rewards for management, early stage investors and later investors can be quite different, leading to difficulty in agreeing a path forward, for example when there is an offer to buy the company. I want to make two recommendations, one general and one specific. The general one is that over the life of the start-up, fostering a deep collegiality between board members is important. This happens at board meetings themselves, especially if there is time for discussions, and the chair encourages everyone to express their views, debate, and achieve consensus. Collegiality is also built outside of board meetings. When board members spend a couple of hours together travelling to and from a meeting site, they learn more about each other's interests and motivations. All this is useful even if it is not enough, hence my more specific recommendation. Because reward is deeply structural in start-up companies, I think it is essential that every time there is a funding round, members have a discussion about what is going to be achieved at this stage of the company, and what would that imply for the next stage. Is there a consensus around when to exit, or even that we are never looking to exit? Because board alignment is crucial to start-up success, achieving consensus early, restating this consensus as things progress, and working to understand where a problem might occur, can be instrumental in averting a clash later.

I have already commented on assessing and understanding risk as a key role of the board, and how often the board fails to do this effectively. One way to make this more useful for both the leadership of the company and the board is to pick out a particular aspect of risk and devote time at a board meeting to that, rather than the more usual approach of scheduling a comprehensive risk discussion every six months. The board might discuss competitors in depth at one meeting, diversity in the customer base (so avoiding the risks associated with one big customer) at another meeting, regulatory risk at yet another. This approach gives focus to the risk discussion, which it often lacks. When effectively managed by the chair, it leads to substantive actions that can be taken and followed up.

All of these things are components of good behaviour on the part of individual board members, the Chair doing their job well, and the board as a whole working together for the success of the company. Perhaps the best way of summarizing what it means is that what we want from the board is wisdom, grown from diverse experience of individuals, including the wisdom of how to work together effectively. Boards that operate from a foundation of wisdom can add tremendous value, and repeatedly help a company avert failure.

REMEMBER THIS TO IMPROVE YOUR CHANCE OF SUCCESS

➤ Aspire to have a better board than your company deserves at its early stage. This does not mean getting famous names, but people who bring diverse experience and a lot of wisdom.

➤ The most essential thing for any board is that it be aligned in its objectives for the company. Spend time on ensuring this alignment, especially after each funding round.

➤ The board's job is governance. Do not wait to install proper governance, especially in key areas like remuneration and audit.

➤ Board time is precious. Spend as much as possible on strategy and risk. The Chair must ensure that these discussions explore difficult issues in depth, and that all voices are heard.

➤ A key role for the Board Chair is as mentor to the CEO; likewise the Chair of the Audit Committee should act as mentor to the CFO. Choose people who can perform these roles effectively.

➤ Just as leadership competencies at the management level must evolve as the company grows, the board should also be evolving so as to meet the different needs of the company.

Notes

1 '278 of the Biggest, Costliest Startup Failures of All Time', CBInsights, 29 August 2023, www.cbinsights.com/research/biggest-startup-failures/, accessed 20 April 2025.

8

The Sixth Cause of Failure

Money or the Lack of It

Dotted through history there are examples of companies that were built from the germ of an idea to a big company without having to ask for money in exchange for part ownership of the business. Historically this happened for small businesses in towns or cities where there was a relationship with a local banker, perhaps receiving a loan to the business in exchange for security on a home, farm or other asset. One of the most famous cases that we know today is Ikea, leaving all the equity remaining with the business founder, Ingvar Kamprad. Microsoft only took very small amounts of venture capital.

Except for businesses whose aim is to provide consulting services in some industrial segment, this reliance on a small loan has pretty much disappeared, particularly for the kind of businesses we are considering in this book, for several reasons. First, the amounts of money required are large, and generally exceed the value of the founder's personal property. Second, the small town banker who saw it as their mission to invest in the local community is gone. Third, founders are generally less concerned with maintaining 100 per cent ownership. Rather, some degree of control, alongside sufficient ownership to provide rewards for success, is paramount in founder thinking. And fourth, as already discussed at the outset of this book, a whole new ecosystem for funding technology start-ups has emerged around the world, that works, in principle, for founders, investors in the companies, and the people with money who back the investors.

There is a version of the local banker that is certainly not universal, though it exists in many localities. This is a government funded entity that has a mission to invest in a country or often in a region. UK examples are Development Bank Wales, investing in businesses in Wales and its Scotland counterpart, Scottish Enterprise. When such organizations function well, they know how to invest taxpayer money so as to simultaneously help fledgling companies while supporting the local economy.

Why is money ever a source of failure unless you need it and don't have it? To get at an answer to this question we are going to revisit the stages of funding a company, and then look at where the problems occur, and how these can be avoided or at least mitigated.

Fundraising: The Different Stages Revisited

There are several distinct stages of raising funds:

- Perhaps scraping together some initial money from friends and family or rich Uncle Charlie.

- Angel investors, particularly groups of high-net-worth individuals who are interested in early-stage companies.

- The special case of angel investors known as crowdfunding, where numerous individuals invest small amounts.

- Proper series A funding, a venture capital firm, or often several of them together, put a substantial chunk of money into the start-up.

- And from there, series B, C, D rounds until the company is viable on its own, or becomes a public company, or is acquired or fails.

Within these there are some exceptional cases or variants worth noting, including the regional investment entities that might participate at angel or other early stage, investment from corporate venture capital groups, or direct investment from corporations with an interest in the technology. All of this is about equity. I am also going to return to talking about debt later in this chapter. With the stage set, we can start to look at money as the cause of failure.

Analytic or Self-Deceiving

The start-up literature is full of articles, blog posts, and book chapters about how to pitch your company to investors. These pearls of wisdom often tell you what the investors are looking for, what will kill your chances of raising money in the first two minutes, how many slides to have or not have.

What they don't usually tell you is about being self-critical as to the possibilities for the business. Often just the opposite, they say that you need to show real ambition, convince the investors this is going to be a 'really big thing'. As a result, just about every slide presentation says something like 'we are at no revenues to speak of today, however we have a lot of interest from customers A, B, and possibly even C, meaning we will have a million in revenue next year, then 10 million, then 100 million'. A common rationale for this, which is a good underpinning for failure, is to say that this is easy. The market is x billion a year (where x is a number greater than 1) and we just have to get 1 per cent of this market to have a big business.

This is not critical thinking. If the investors are dumb enough to be convinced by that approach, well, they deserve to lose all their money. Most often they will think, 'these people just are not being analytic about the market they are trying to penetrate'.

This approach to explaining the market becomes a source of failure when **the founders** actually believe it. You have now passed from the realm of salesmanship (to the investors) to self-deception. In fact, what you must believe is that it is difficult for every single new product to find traction in the market and grow into a substantial cash generative business. That is why you need to be analytic about this, not because a potential investor is telling you to be. Still, you need to have and convey sufficient self-belief that, difficult as this is, you can and will achieve it.

The Trap of Raising Too Little

As an angel investor, I am regularly presented with pitches from companies seeking to raise £500,000. Okay, this is an early-stage company, and perhaps that will get them from where they are today to the next milestone. This funding goal often comes after a description of the product or service, and their ambitions for the coming eighteen months. Usually, it is clear that £500,000 is not going to get them there. So why are they asking for that amount? As a founder trying to raise money, have you thought about whether there is a logic that underpins your ask?

Perhaps the best reason for raising less than you need is that you are a first time entrepreneur, and you don't think that investors will risk more than that on you at this early stage of your business. You might be right. However, these investors are savvy enough to know that you will not go off with £500,000, accomplish all your goals and then be back in say, fifteen months, looking for £5 million to get to the next stage. What they know is that you will be back in six months looking for another £500,000.

Well, if that is the best reason, the worst reason for raising too little is that you and those who helped you get started currently own 100 per cent of the company, and you know that at its current value (valuation, see later) to raise what you really need, say £2 million, you would have to give away 60 per cent, and you just don't want to do that. As a result of this thinking, your tactic (calling it a strategy would be a mistake) is to raise a small amount, use that to get the valuation up, raise another small amount, rinse and repeat, all the while maintaining your share.

This is a long and winding road to failure. You can't hire the best people, or even the minimum number of people you need, because you don't have enough money. The product, be it hardware or software, goes from an early stage to something slightly better that is still not convincing. If you are a somewhat experienced business person, there are things you know you should be doing to build a foundation for the success of the company; you don't do them because the cash just isn't there.

What have you done? You have maintained your ownership share in a small company, and as a result you have a large piece of a small pie. What you really want is a small, but still significant piece of a much bigger pie. By raising too little, you have started the company on the road to failure through penury.

Shortage of Cash Leads to False Economies

When you raise only a small amount of money, you need to be disciplined about every cent you spend. Now that is a good thing. Sometimes start-ups that raise a big early round of funding don't have that discipline and dissipate the cash advantage they have. How does having too little money at the early stage become a failure trap?

In any early-stage company there are certain necessary costs: leading the company, the salaries and incentives to the key people building the product so it can be truly commercial (or more likely the stage before commercial), overhead costs, such as space rental, basic accounting services. Founders should know they can't skimp on these or they will never survive to get to the next stage.

What about the intellectual property being created? Intellectual property is the embodiment of a big part of the value of any early-stage company. You don't yet have customers, or even a minimum viable product, your brand is not known. What you do have are inventions, maybe some original use for an existing technology, ways of building things and making them work, maybe even an original name or image. It is important that this intellectual property be protected, through patents, trademarks, copyright, trade secrets. Doing this right, with, for example a proper firm of attorneys who will help you document everything, write patents where appropriate, file these, extend them to different jurisdictions, is essential at this stage. It costs money, and you look at these costs and decide that they can't be justified from the shrinking small cash pile you have. As a result, intellectual property protection becomes 'something we will do later', even though investors in 'later' see it as a crucial thing they are buying. As a founder you were right to say you can't afford this, but wrong to have raised too small an amount of money to be able to afford it.

Another crucial early stage thing that gets ignored is marketing. Founders think that the essential thing to demonstrate is some early sales, and I am not dismissing this as being unimportant. Too often they jump right to sales and ignore marketing. Marketing is about creating awareness of the product and its distinctiveness. It lays the foundation for sales, shapes and builds the brand, creates demand for the product. In earlier times this was done through advertising, trade shows, things that were quite expensive and often out of reach of a start-up, even a well-funded one. Now there are much more efficient ways to reach the market, with the fundamentals of an attractive, informative website, various social networks and online newsletters, podcasts and so on. Sure, face to face at a trade conference with 10,000 attendees is great, but you may not be ready for that anyway. Still, even with efficient use of technological tools for marketing, it takes money. If you have raised too little you can't afford to do your early stage marketing, so you opt for a few low value sales instead. A fundamental building block of competitive advantage is sacrificed.

I have already mentioned the importance to a start-up company of a proper CFO. This is probably not something that any company with just a small pool of money can afford, and I am not advocating it. However, as soon as you get to one more leg up the funding ladder there will be advantages to having this role in house. Companies that have been used to living with very small amounts of cash, always seeing the month where they will run out looming before them, have trouble changing their mindset when a somewhat bigger funding round has happened. You are not rich, but you do have to move the company to its next stage, and a CFO is important in making this happen. More on this later in the chapter.

Failure Through Constant Fundraising

What is the fundraising consequence of the trap I have just described, wherein you raise a small amount of money, effectively enough to see you through the next six months rather than what you really need: two years of what is known as 'runway'?

It means that as a founder you are going back to the current and potential investors again in four months to ask for more money. This involves meetings where you pitch what little has been accomplished, go through yet more due diligence, especially with new investors, deal with lawyers ... all of which is costly in money, which you are short of, and your time as founder, which is the thing of which you are most short.

This is time you should have been spending running the business, marketing the company and its products, talking to potential customers or getting feedback from early adopters, lining up partners for helping to get your product to market – the list goes on. Instead, you are worrying about exactly when you will not be able to pay your hard working staff, and yourself, and answering endless questions from the people you need to fund the next stage.

Have you learned your lesson? Are you going back and saying, 'look, we took £500,000, have accomplished a lot in a short time. Now we need £2.5 million to get this thing really launched'? Too often as an angel investor I have seen that this lesson is not learned, and that the same mentality applies, 'Here we are again, please can we have another £500,000?'

One of the failings of angel investor networks is that they don't sufficiently discourage this bad behaviour. Having invested in the start-up, they now have an advantageous position, and perhaps they get into the mindset of the founders, namely, *they* want to maintain *their* percentage ownership of the small pie rather than get the company adequately funded. They are now board members who can be holding the company back instead of propelling it forward.

By sticking with angel investors too long, founders condemn themselves to slow rates of progress, which can allow better funded competitors to grab the lead in the market. At an early stage, speed may not be everything, but it is a particularly important thing. Without sufficient funds, and by constantly fundraising, speed is also sacrificed.

One other aspect to this problem is worth talking about here, and that is investor commitment. When a company is ready to move from angel investors to proper venture capital investment, and fails to do so, it is depriving itself of more than just the larger sums of money. There is a level of ambition and experience that comes from a good/great venture firm that means the probability of failure is greatly reduced. Even the questions that will be explored during the fundraising and due diligence process will bring up issues of consequence for success. I am not saying that angel investors are unsophisticated. In my experience they are usually particularly good business people, and often technically knowledgeable. They are also committed to helping entrepreneurs succeed. Just recognize they are doing this part-time. They turn up once every couple of months, spend a little time listening, maybe participate in some due diligence, and then write a cheque. Full time partners in a venture firm have a completely different kind of commitment. After a few years of working at it they should have a different level of expertise in how to make start-ups succeed.

For all these reasons it is good for an early-stage company to make the transition from angel investing to venture funds as soon as it can get their attention.

Valuation: Neither Art Nor Science?

A company, even one just founded by two people, Jack and Jill, in a dorm room, is worth something. There is an idea, there are two smart people, often they will have done some work before they start a company. How much is it worth? What is its valuation?

Well, that is a hard question to answer at effectively zero stage. Perhaps it doesn't matter at that point. If the two are working on a software product, they can spend time developing it to a prototype stage and get some of their university mates to try it out. Now it is getting some traction, they know what features they must add, what is not working so well, and they also know that they need help, or at least helpers. To afford these helpers they want to raise some money.

Following on from my earlier discussion about not wanting to give away too much of the company, so raising too little money, we now have a different lens on the same problem. Suppose Jack and Jill decide they need $1 million to get this business going, the question they are asking is what per cent of the business are we willing to give away for that million? If they assert that the business is, even at this early stage, worth $3 million, then that is its 'pre-money' (i.e. pre the $1 million injection) valuation, and after the fundraising, if they are successful, they own 75 per cent of the business, which has a post money valuation of $4 million.

The investors of the $1 million are also asking questions about the valuation. First and foremost, is there anything that justifies the $3 million number? Immediately thereafter, they are thinking about the future, and what does this business have to be worth in the long term for me to make a return on my $1 million? The higher the valuation at this early stage, the bigger the company needs to become for the investors to make an acceptable return. If you are a venture investor putting in something like $20 million in an early round, and there is a $100 million post money valuation, there will be an investment committee discussion along the lines of:

> Well, there will be a couple of more rounds, because it is going to take a lot more capital to get this business up to scale. If each time the valuation goes up by 2x, soon we are close to a billion dollar company, which I like, but now the late stage investors will need to sell or IPO the company for at least 3x the previous valuation in order to get a return on their investment. Can I possibly see this little business ever being worth that much?

Now we are in a founder's dilemma. If the valuation is too low, either you must give away a lot of the company to raise the money you need, or you can only raise a small amount. If the valuation is high, and you can convince investors that this high valuation is justified, you can raise more money. You will have to live with the expectations of the investors being much higher.

Exactly the same problem comes throughout the life of a venture backed company. There are pressures to drive pre-money valuation up, even if doing so increases the risk of the company doing things that are not in its best interest. Rather they are being driven by the needs of the investors.

Valuation is a Goldilocks problem. Set it too low, and you are not giving yourself credit for what you have achieved. You will also not be able to raise sufficient funds for the next stage. Set it too high and you are on a treadmill to justifying a billion-dollar exit, which might necessitate actions that are inconsistent with building a sound, sustainable business.

Founders coming from technical backgrounds, and many do, have trouble recognizing this sort of problem. They assume that business must have rules and formulas that allow you to calculate something as fundamental as valuation. Sadly, no such formulas exist. Investors try to look at comparable companies, and base their assessment on those, while founders will argue that the whole idea of this company is that it is completely disruptive, so there are no comparables. Angel investors are even less scientific, they just say things like, 'I don't like investing in something with $x million valuation,' and they are partly right, because it becomes hard for them to get a decent return on their investment.

How do we optimize for success and minimize failure in this situation? I prefer to keep valuations low to moderate at early stages and give away a bigger share of the company to raise the money that is needed. This is consistent with my views in the previous section. Then, if real progress is made, drive the valuations up faster with successive fundraising, because you can show that this is justified.

Money From the Government: Non-Dilutive Funding or Distraction From Goal?

Many countries, sometimes regions within countries, are trying to encourage technology entrepreneurship. I have already mentioned the possibility of direct investment by government entities as part of a fundraising. At an early stage, there can also be direct government grants to early-stage companies.

The government grant system for science as we know it is really a World War II and post war invention. It was designed to support universities as well as to create government labs, the former doing basic research and the latter some basic research, more applied research, always with a well-defined mission. In the US this grew out of the Department of Defense, then led to the creation of the National Science Foundation and National Institutes of Health, the large Department of Energy Labs such as Los Alamos, Oak Ridge, Lawrence

Livermore and Argonne, as well as NASA labs. In the UK, the structure involves Research Councils making grants across a wide range of disciplines, as well as various government labs. France has the CNRS, Canada a wide-ranging grant structure.

A more recent development has been the idea of making grants to start-up companies, with a view to creating a meaningful business position in certain technological areas. As a consequence, the UK Research Councils were renamed as UK Research and Innovation, and a part of their mission became 'to help companies to grow through their development and commercialization of new products, processes and services, supported by an outstanding innovation ecosystem that is agile, inclusive and easy to navigate'. In the US, the National Science Foundation has created 'America's Seed Fund', which can make grants of up to $2 million to deep tech start-up companies. These grants do not involve taking equity in the companies that are funded.

Is this the ideal funding source for a start-up company? It has the advantage of injecting valuable cash without diluting ownership for either founders or external investors. And it's patriotic, besides! So, what's the problem, or why be cautious?

The most important question I always ask as an investor or board member about grant funding is this: Is the company receiving a grant to support the work that it really wants to do? Let's put it this way. The founders go to external investors – angels, venture groups, whatever – and say give us this money and over the next two years we will go from a prototype product to something that has these additional features, and is manufacturable at 40 per cent less than what we can do today, with very high reliability, meeting this need in the market. Fine. Now they go to the government entity funding small companies and say give us a grant to do these things. Maybe the answer is 'yes', in which case no problem. In my experience, sometimes the answer is, 'well, we don't really provide funding for things like lowering cost and improving reliability, but you also have the possibility of showing that your device/program/service can work in other areas as well, and we would love to fund the research and development to make that happen'.

Now you are still getting the money, unfortunately it is for something that is far down on the priority list. It looks good, there is $2 million of non-dilutive funding, but is it advancing the business? Worse, are you taking the precious talent you need to get to a robust, winning product and diverting it to something else?

Government grants also involve a process of application, review, usually payment on a reimbursement basis rather than up front, accounting on various government forms, so can be both a cashflow problem and entail increased overheads. Companies must be realistic about the direct and indirect costs of government funding.

Another wrinkle is a mixing of the company's mission with other aims that the government is trying to accomplish. Besides helping you get your business going, the government agency wants to support and encourage aspects of more applied research at universities. You apply for the grant, and they say, great, but why don't you also involve the excellent research group at the University of Wherever? Maybe this group can really help you advance your product. More often it will just mean another management and accounting task, another loss of focus with no benefit. Do you really want to take a grant if this is your assessment of what it will entail?

This sounds negative. I want it to be more cautionary than negative. If you can get government funds to do what you want to do, what you really need to do, great. If it is going to distract you from your goals, involve you in a lot of additional time and coordination, think twice before taking it. In general, I would say that start-up boards should have to agree all applications for government funding to make sure there is a sound business case to contribute to the company's success.

Money From The Government: Industrial Policy as a Trap

When government decides to fund start-ups to build the base of strong technology businesses it can do a lot of good. If you are leading this effort in the government, why stop with such a simple goal? Rather, you think you should impose on it some of your great wisdom about what the most fruitful areas are for development, so you study these, get some experts in, and as a result announce that you are going to support start-up companies in Quantum Computing, Hydrogen Fuel Cells, Large Learning Models, and Advanced Semiconductor devices. Sounds reasonable? After all, these are all fashionable areas, and getting a lot of press coverage, so it must make sense to choose them for investment.

Government has now created the start-up roots of an industrial policy, and it is using its funds to encourage other investors to put their money into certain areas. The amounts of money government can muster behind such initiatives can be large and so exert a disproportionate influence on what gets funded. Well, the government leadership who has created this policy say, 'that is exactly what we are trying to do'. It works, it definitely moves the money, and we have seen this across several areas over many decades. The only problem comes when they are wrong.

A drunken man comes out of a bar, which happens to be next to a river. If he has no idea how to get home, he wanders first this way and that way. He may or may not get home before he falls asleep, but at least the chance of his falling into the river is small. However, if he has a theory about how to get home, and that theory is wrong, he is going right into the river!

If the wise people of government and their advisers support a whole bunch of technological areas, or just choose companies that they think are credible, there is a good chance of some successes. The money invested will boost the impact of other investors and give a good return to the economy of the country.

If they choose three areas to support, and those are the wrong areas – right into the river! If you are an investor alongside government in this adventure, you may not drown but you will certainly get very wet.

Working Capital: Not Knowing What You Don't Know

Founders working on their first business have usually not had any business education. They may have a PhD in Physics or Biotechnology, and as a result think business is pretty simple. In fact, it is pretty simple, though there is more to it than the Micawber Principle, 'Annual income twenty pounds, annual expenditure nineteen and six, result happiness. Annual income twenty pounds, annual expenditure twenty pounds nought and six, result misery.'

So far, we have talked about fundraising to support salaries, office and lab space, equipment required (whether that is just computers or other more complex laboratory or manufacturing equipment). In general, these needs justify giving equity in the company to investors. Once you have raised this capital and made one time expenditures, you can see how much cash you have, how fast you are spending it (the burn rate) and predict when it will run out in various projections of the income and margin from sales. At later stages, and we will come to this, equity might be raised to acquire other companies.

There is one important thing not covered by these general categories of expenditure, however. Suppose you are making electronic devices that you are going to sell to end customers, either businesses or consumers. In these devices there are a number of chips that you must buy from an Asian supplier, various electronic boards and components coming from Germany, a container that houses all of it that you will brand which is made locally and so on. These component parts are likely to have certain characteristics that you might not appreciate until you start to ramp up production: First, they are probably not supplied by Amazon Prime, so you are not going to get next day delivery. Indeed, you might find that some key parts can only be supplied in ninety days, or even longer. Second, the price varies a lot by how many you buy. If you buy 1 chip it might cost five times as much as if you buy 100, and the factor could be much larger at higher quantities. While you don't have to make the devices with a 'cost of goods' of the exceptionally large quantities, you can't afford to do it with the cost of a single chip either.

As a business leader, you must forecast your sales, of course. That's routine though difficult for a start-up. You also must build up your stock of parts so that you can meet demand when it comes, and meet that demand at a cost that still leaves you with the possibility of making enough money so you don't go out of business. All of this becomes a part of what is known as the working capital of the business. I have yet to find a science PhD programme that teaches its students about working capital.

A business of this sort must build up its inventory of component parts well ahead of getting in revenue from sales. The faster the sales ramp you are seeing, the more you must build up this inventory, so the more money you have to pay to suppliers. Since you are a small start-up business, the suppliers may demand payment in advance, or immediately on delivery. By contrast, even after you have delivered your gadgets to the larger businesses who are your customers you may have to wait sixty days to get paid.

Most founders don't appreciate the magnitude of this problem. It is not complicated, it doesn't require a PhD in Physics to understand it, but if you have never faced it before it can hit you hard. You have just raised money from investors with the promise of the ramp in sales, you are getting that traction, and yet you don't have the cash required to meet the demand in a timely fashion.

I think it is easy to see how this can become a failure mode, for a company that is otherwise being successful and doing everything right. I will discuss the way out of it at the end of this chapter. Suffice to say that usually the efficient way out is to not give away more equity to fund working capital but to borrow the money, that is, take on debt.

How hard is this solution going to be to implement? Well, that depends. If you have a handful of purchase orders for your devices there are probably several sources of debt that can help you out in the short term, at reasonable interest rates and terms. If things are not quite so certain, and that is often the case, it may be more difficult to secure.

Later Stage Investment Failure Modes

A lot of this discussion has focused on early stage investment, and the early stages of a company. That is probably the right emphasis, because the largest number of failures happen at this stage, and even if they don't, it is when the structural flaws which lead to the failures are built into the company. Still, once the rocket seems to be launched, the business has some scale and the valuation has reached an attractive if not stratospheric number, how can fundraising still lead to new failure modes?

How's this for a case history? Miasolé is a solar module company using a different chemistry from conventional silicon solar cells. I quote here from the Wikipedia page on its fundraising history:

> MiaSolé's initial raise was in 2004 and led by VantagePoint Venture Partners. The B round raised $16 million in venture capital investment in June 2005, in a round led by Kleiner Perkins Caufield & Byers, and raised a further $35 million in October 2006. The company raised $50 million in a fourth round of financing in September 2007, bringing total financing to $100 million. MiaSolé (eventually had) $500 million in investment from investors including VantagePoint Venture Partners, Kleiner Perkins, and Firelake Capital Management. In addition, the company received about $100 million

federal tax credit from the United States Department of Energy. On January 9, 2013, Hanergy issued a press release stating that it had acquired MiaSolé for $30 million.[1]

By the time it was acquired, Miasolé had reached a valuation of well over a billion dollars. The venture capital firms that invested in it are, or were, big, sophisticated firms, yet they continued to pour in money. Firelake invested in 2012, when the company's valuation was already extremely high. Miasolé is far from an isolated example. I have already mentioned the case of Better Place, launched in 2007, which by 2011 had raised $700 million, again from sophisticated investors, and filed for bankruptcy in 2013.

There are many reasons for these failures, and I have already discussed some of them in earlier chapters. What I want to highlight here is the connection of failure to multiple rounds of fundraising at progressively higher valuations. What we have is a built-in problem of alignment, or the lack thereof. There are often issues of alignment between the investor directors on the board and the founders. This problem can also show up in considerations of how different venture firms are going to get a return on their investment (of money and effort) when some investors come into the company at a very high valuation whereas others, also represented on the board, have acquired at least some of their shares at much lower valuations.

In this situation, there can be an inherent mismatch on what is the right thing for the company to do next. For a company that is becoming mature, having an impact on an industry or a market, at this stage it is possible that one or more unsolicited offers come through to acquire the company. Are the board members at this late stage asking, 'What is best for our company?' or are they only asking, 'What is best for my investment?' When it is the latter, it becomes a failure mode. If I could draw a looping arrow at this point the arrow would point back to the end of the previous chapter on boards as a source of failure, and once again urge the Chair to see if it is possible to get alignment.

Maybe it isn't, in which case at least go into the later funding round with eyes wide open, because that is always the best way to avoid traps.

It's Not Always About Money, but Often it is. Get This Right

The biggest positive lesson I want to draw from this discussion of funding and failure is that companies need money to develop, grow, and have impact. Usually, they need more money than they admit, and they need it sooner. Sure, taking this money means giving up both founders' share in the company, and their control. It may even mean that the investors one day decide that the founders are not the right people to be leading the company in its next stage. If you are going to be successful you have to accept all of this, because you believe that there is a bigger prize.

Funding happens in the sorts of stages I have described, and these are discrete events. Looking for the funding may take time, then you get an offer, legal documents are prepared, and one day there is money in the bank account. For most start-ups, every one of these funding rounds is a struggle, certainly at the early stages of pre-revenue or low revenue, managing the tension between visibility of the date when you will no longer have enough cash and the date the money comes in. When a company is established, having timely funding means that it is possible to carry out planned expansion, add key staff, perhaps make an acquisition. It may not be the same sort of angst that you have when worrying about whether you can meet a payroll, but founders care deeply about their company and being able to execute on opportunities. I would say to investors at all stages, yes, you are (often) entrusted with investing other people's money, and you need to do your diligence; you don't always need to prolong negotiations and legal work for as many weeks or months as often happens.

Let's turn to the tricky subject of valuation: what is the company worth to a new investor, which in turn translates into what share of the company you are acquiring for your investment. Raising money, particularly with aggressive start-up founders and arrogant venture capitalists, can become a macho struggle in which each side is seeking a win, rather than what it should be, a beginning of a relationship designed to build something of value for both parties and for the customers of the company. I believe that approaching this in the positive mode of relationship building is going to increase the ultimate chance of success. Both parties must start this relationship by looking at pre-money valuation as serious business people, not as a game. If an investor is treating you in an insulting and abusive manner over valuation, and I have seen this happen, then that is probably how they are going to treat you once they own a share of the company and sit on the board. You don't want to be in a relationship with such a firm.

Ultimately, the valuation is whatever an investor is willing to pay for a share of the company. Although ChatGPT will give you formulas that make sense if you have significant revenues, and work better if you are generating more cash than you are spending, let's agree that calculating valuation is not a science where the formula can tell you the answer, while we also agree that there needs to be some logic, a consideration of facts, as well as how hot the market is – both for the product and for investment. The obligation is on the start-up to say to potential investors what they believe the valuation is, using a number they can defend with a logical basis. Then the investor can negotiate, also from logic, or can say, 'I wish you well, but I just can't get to that sort of valuation'.

For later stage companies, just running the valuation up to a billion dollars does not mean that if you own 10 per cent of it you have a bankable $100 million. It might, of course it might. You still must do the hard work, of course avoiding failure, because the ultimate exit valuation is the only thing that is important.

Thus far, I have been discussing money in terms of equity. It is not the only choice. In helping companies be successful while keeping them funded appropriately, everyone, boards and executives, should understand when debt is better than equity, and when it is worse. As with equity valuation, people understandably prefer not to reduce their share of ownership, and debt is one way to accomplish this. Especially attractive can be loans either directly from government agencies or from banks where the government guarantees all or part of the debt. The attraction here is that someone other than the bank is taking all or most of the risk, which means that the approval process, while still rigorous, will have a higher chance of success than debt directly funded from a bank or other financial entity. Government's appetite for risk, and their motivations for extending or guaranteeing a loan, are quite different from that of a modern bank.

Interacting with these government entities and their banking partners requires a degree of sophistication, and this will work best when the presentation of the company is done by the senior executives, who convey the excitement behind the venture, while the negotiations are done by a proper CFO of the company. The terms of a loan can have a big impact down the road in the outcomes for the start-up. Why? Because often on exit/sale of the company the debt will be the first thing that gets paid, before any of the shareholders. The CFO and the board need to appreciate what is being committed and take a realistic view of the ability to manage the debt, both interest and principal, over the course of its term.

Earlier I have stressed the importance of working capital funding to start-up success. Start-ups should be very aware of government and bank programmes specifically designed for this.[2] These can be particularly attractive when the product is being made largely for export, taking advantage of the fact that governments are not only encouraging technology companies but trying to strengthen economic competitiveness. Programmes like UK Export Finance are designed to do just that.

None of these debt instruments can be secured in a week or even a month. They involve presentations, committees, champions in the government agencies, careful organization of information. As always, companies that do detailed financial planning and have a strong executive team will be the ones that succeed in the process.

Another source of cash can be credits from the government for research you have done[3]. The amounts involved can be quite material to an early-stage company, you just need to keep careful records and be adept at completing the required forms, being sure that you get it right the first time. With good financial staff, either internally or as advisers, it should be possible to know how much you can receive and when you will receive it with considerable accuracy.

Now that most common phrasal question you will hear in the workplace and boardroom of start-ups is, 'What is your burn rate?' Funding has been raised, staff has been hired, space has been rented, and now you are spending thousands of pounds/dollars/euros a month. That is the burn rate. At this rate, when will you run out of cash? These items, staff cost, space costs, are in your control. On the other side of the ledger is revenue from sales, grants, tax credits. Of these, the sales revenue is the least controllable item, whether it is first sales, a ramp up that you are counting on, or later stage progress. Companies can succeed by being very thoughtful about staffing in the early stages. Even if you know what you need to succeed, how much of it you can afford and when can you afford it is a crucial decision. Does this seem obvious? Sure, but the leadership, probably with help and advice from the board, needs to make the decisions, which will almost always involve compromise. To succeed, those compromises need to be more about quantity than quality. A lot of second or third rate staff are not going to yield the progress that a few more expensive first rate ones will.

REMEMBER THIS TO IMPROVE YOUR CHANCE OF SUCCESS

- Start-ups will always need more money than you think. When funding is available, try to get the maximum possible, even when it means giving up a big share of your company. Everything takes longer than expected in starting a business, and you can't fix problems if you are broke.

- Multiple rounds of fundraising take time and effort, and you have to expect that these also will go on longer than you expect. Try to get good investors who have the resources to continue to back you. Be thoughtful about valuation when approaching investors. It is your obligation as a founder to have a good, logical defence of your proposed valuation.

- Government funding, when available, can be a major support, but only if it helps you to stay on the road to achieving your main goals. It also gives a certain kind of credibility, and possibly some useful publicity. Never let it distract you or cause you to lose focus.

- Debt funding can be particularly valuable. Look for government-backed loan programmes, especially if they help you fund working capital requirements.

- Ultimately, what matters is cash!

Notes

1. 'Miasolé', Wikipedia, https://en.wikipedia.org/wiki/Miasolé, accessed 3 April 2025.
2. An example is UK Export Finance, ukexportfinance.gov.uk.
3. For the UK example, which has some excellent definitions and explanations, see 'Check If You Can Claim Research & Development (R&D) Tax Relief', UK Government, www.gov.uk/guidance/corporation-tax-research-and-development-rd-relief, accessed 27 April 2025.

9

This, That, and the Other Thing

There sure are a lot of ways to fail, and most of them are avoidable, or at the very least the risk of going down one of these failure paths can be mitigated. I have already discussed the six that I think are the biggest and made several suggestions about how to deal with them. Now I want to pick up on a number of others that come up from time to time, and are worth giving conscious attention, at least something like a little red flag that appears in your peripheral vision when an issue like this starts to rear its ugly head.

Focus, Pivot, or Quit

I am a great believer in focus. Bright people overflow with ideas. Many of the founders of technology start-ups are at least thinking, if not saying to their investors, this is the first thing we are going to build and sell, and it will be great, but there are five others that I will get to as soon as this one gets going. The slippery slope from this thinking is having two of your precious few staff working on idea number two, because you want it to advance while the rest of us are working on main idea number one. Then this skunkworks on idea two also consumes 20 per cent of the founder's time, because he has a bit of passion for it. All of this is lack of focus, and it reduces the chance of success.

I think most people would agree that relentless focus on achieving the first thing is crucial. For most start-ups this is the recommended course of action, until it isn't. Because. . . it doesn't always work. Yes, the first users loved the app, unfortunately they were not typical of the mass market, and sales are just not happening. Still, we learned and now we can see a bigger opportunity based on market response. Maybe there has been a change in the regulatory space and a new opportunity opens that was previously not significant. For whatever reason, idea number two now starts to take a bigger mindshare. It has many of the features that idea one had, perhaps it is a bit more 'downmarket', and might appeal to the general user rather than the specialist. Is this the time for the company to continue to **focus** on making idea one work, *or* should it **pivot** to number two? In looking at this choice, it is always good to keep in mind that a pivot is going to be difficult; it's not a straightforward way out of your problems.

Another focus or pivot question can occur around geography. All the effort in the early days of the company has been on your home market, which makes sense. You know it well, know who to talk to, where to network for early sales. At some point you learn, maybe through getting a few users in another country, that there is a bigger and more easily accessible market for your product. Perhaps, in a technology trying to solve an environmental problem, the regulatory climate in another country is better aligned with what you are trying to accomplish. You don't have the resources for both, but is it time to continue focusing on the home market, or pivot to the new one?

Lack of focus is one of the most common causes of failure, but failure to pivot when all the signs say pivot in big bold letters can also be fatal. If this seems like a hard, or almost impossible decision to make, then that is because life in start-up world is filled with almost impossible choices.

I have presented the choice here as focus or pivot. Entrepreneurs have another more difficult choice to make. When focusing on the initial product/market is clearly not going to work, the choice becomes 'pivot or quit'. For almost every start-up there is a day when you must ask yourself whether it would be best to make the hard choice to give up on this business. Maybe that is shut it down, maybe sell the intellectual property to someone who might make use of it. In these circumstances, pivot might not be a successful alternative to focus, but a way of avoiding the right decision, to quit.

International Expansion

Having touched on the difficult decision of whether to pivot to a new geography, it is worth looking at the related question of expanding into more countries, international expansion. If the start-up is in the US, or China or India, and was designed for one of those markets, you might say that you have a pretty big field to conquer before going to another country, if you ever do. If you are a founder in Sweden, or Switzerland, for example, you could quickly run out of the potential for growth and scale.

There are few products that can successfully transfer from the country in which they were founded to another country without a bit of adaptation. Yes, both the UK and the US are English speaking, but boy do they see products differently. Pursuing other markets involves more than just hiring a salesperson or creating a website with a different currency for payments. All of this takes learning and effort. If you are not willing and able to put in this effort, the new market will be a failure and drain resources from the company.

When it is clear, probably from the outset, that a company is going to have to go beyond its home market in order to succeed at scale, planning, timing, and ability to devote the required resources to the new market are crucial to avoiding failure.

Founder Relationships

Are you sure you want to found a company together with your spouse, your sister, or your grandfather for that matter? The relationships we have with our 'nearest and dearest' are very different from those with whom we work. Let's put aside the complex of issues that arise when romance develops in the workplace. Here I just want to consider the question of starting, and investing, in a company where the founders have a relationship other than business partner.

Starting and leading a new company is a lonely and difficult thing. Many experienced entrepreneurs say that it has been useful, even essential, for them to have a co-founder with whom they share the good and bad times, especially on the most difficult days and weeks. While supporting this advice, it is not the same as having a co-founder with whom you have a relationship other than work. Even without the added complexity of relationships, there are many cases of co-founders struggling to stay together. Finding ways to collaborate under stress is just hard.

Historically, the family firm was the bedrock of capitalist society. This was usually about the men in the family, with fathers taking in their sons as they matured. While we can call to mind the great enduring firms of extended families, like the Rothschilds, the fact is that most family firms don't survive beyond three generations. There are just too many diverse needs and priorities that lead to the firm being sold or closed.

My fellow angel investors and I were recently looking at a firm that had what looked like promising new technology. The founders were both young men, and quite complementary in their competencies – one being a great technical founder and the clear brains behind the technology, the other being the more astute salesman. Okay, they needed to add serious engineering expertise to turn the clever science into a product, but we knew how to help them with that. We were about three meetings in with the founders when we learned that the two men were in a relationship with each other and had a child together. Nothing wrong with that, though for some of us it raised red flags. Did they think that if we knew this from the outset, we would reject them without considering the business proposition? If so, would we have been wrong? Now I have known married couples who have successfully started, grown, and run a firm together. I just think that we must question whether it is a good idea, and what additional risk of failure is being layered on to all the others by adding this bit of complexity.

This problem of founder relationships can be about more than just founding a company with your siblings or romantic partner/spouse. Sometimes two people who have known each other for several years as friends decide to start a company together. They reason, probably separately coming to the same conclusion, that there is between them trust and respect, meaning that they should be able to work well together in an enterprise that they both are passionate about. They haven't asked themselves, or I would say, dared to ask themselves, who will be in charge. At the beginning it doesn't matter, there are just the two of them trying to tell a story and build an early product. Once there are six or ten employees, it does matter who is deciding to do what. The employees, who probably also have small stakes in the business, want to know whose direction to follow, especially if there are two conflicting messages.

It is a basic maxim of businesses that there needs to be one chief executive, and that having co-CEOs rarely works for any extended period. When there is a relationship, sibling, spouse or long-term friendship between founders, this should be worked out in advance, lest it become a failure mode part way through the growth of the enterprise.

Marketing, Not Just Sales

This bit of the failure discussion could have been discussed under the second cause of failure, though it might have got lost there, where I was talking about the market for a product. The market is a noun; marketing is a verb. When I ask companies about their marketing programme, I often get a response that talks about focusing on getting the first sales, then driving down the cost of acquiring new customers, and eventually building sales to a sustainable level. These are all good goals, but they are not about marketing.

Start-ups sometimes fail because they think only about sales and not about marketing. Marketing involves research, and that research is very much consumer focused, whether it is a retail consumer or a business. How many start-ups spend any time really doing research on who their customer is, or might be, and what they need? Unless you do research on the market you can't properly formulate your offer, you can't educate the market about your offer, learn how the environment you are trying to sell into is changing, educate your customers about your offer, and promote it effectively.

This is not the place to regurgitate a textbook on marketing, and there are many. Rather I just want to emphasize that those leading a start-up tend to think about sales a lot – who are you contacting, what do I have to tell them to get to 'yes', what discount do I have to give and to whom. The boards of these companies always ask to see the sales funnel and rarely ask questions about the marketing programme. When building a business, the entire sales process will be more effective if you have done the work to understand the market, and often the leaders of start-ups don't see the value of this. This is ironic, in a way, because many of the leaders in technology start-ups come from research backgrounds. They would never approach the solution of a scientific or engineering problem the way they approach getting their product adopted by customers.

Once you have a programme of market research it can inform how you position your company vis a vis competitors, be they innovators like yourself or established firms who think they are solving the problem. This 'counter-positioning', which I will discuss further when I talk about strategy, is a crucial way that companies succeed. It only can work based on understanding of the market.

More Involved, More Delegating?

In a new company, everyone works on everything. Yes, you have to trust someone in the group to get a particular job done that they have taken on, but if you are the leader you also have to look at the result, test it, apply your standards of quality and robustness. That is why you are the leader and will be respected.

As the company grows, even a little bit, the leader must make a transition to delegating more of the work to others. It is likely that the head of manufacturing, or the senior engineer, knows a lot more about their job than you do. If you are double checking their work all the time, they will feel a lack of trust, get frustrated, and probably leave. This transition from being deeply involved to delegating accountability is a tough one for all leaders, because it means letting go when you care deeply about the outcome. A growth in maturity of a start-up CEO is knowing who you can trust and who needs more of your involvement.

This is a delicate balance, because as with many aspects of the start-up journey, you are walking a narrow path to success with failure on either side. If you don't delegate enough, you will not have the time to work on things that are important to the business that only you, as CEO can do, while you may lose key specialists. If you trust someone and they don't deliver the quality product you require the business is in danger of failure.

How do successful leaders navigate this path? By being outcomes-focused rather than process-focused. Don't second guess the lead manufacturing guy on who he has assigned to which job, or what priority he has given to fixing which problem. Do ask the right questions about when we will be able to get x units out into the field for testing with customers.

Now suppose we have a product and a small sales team of some sort to get us a few early customers. Does the CEO delegate everything to the sales team, the way I have suggested for manufacturing? In my view, the answer is the complete opposite. The most important thing you can learn as CEO is how customers react to your product. For that, you must see how it is being presented, what features generate excitement, while also learning the features that customers don't seem to really care about. For this you need to be present, at least some of the time, with the sales team when they are in front of customers. Remember, there is a cycle here, of design, manufacture, market, sell, and then close the loop with redesign based on customer feedback. In most start-ups it is only the CEO who can close this loop and generate the constant improvement that makes a company successful in the early stages.

We see that 'delegate or stay involved' is not the choice. It is delegate *and* stay involved. This requires different leadership competencies for distinct stages as well as different aspects of the business. That is why being a leader of a start-up is so difficult.

Boring is Bad, or Good

Many venture investors try to become part of the herd. The excitement today is all about AI, so everyone must have several AI investments in their portfolio. Likewise, founders, particularly first-time founders, think that they need an exciting proposition in a hot area if they are going to get the attention of investors. It is true that the big winners in the exciting areas are the companies that will probably return 100x the investment.

Let's be clear: these exciting, highly disruptive companies are just the sort of companies that are most prone to failure, and this has been true for decades if not centuries. There are all sorts of reasons, including many I have touched on earlier. The most fashionable technology is the one that often attracts charlatans and amateurs, who can tell a good story but not deliver on it. Even when they can make a useable product, many others can do so as well. Utterback's exposition of the 'dominant design' shows the consequence of this with many examples such as typewriters, automobile companies, and the television industry.[1] In each case, the number of firms proliferated, then a dominant design emerged, and there was a collapse to a small number, sometimes only two. This model continues to be valid for every frontier technology today.

With businesses that are a bit more boring, for example companies that can do everything required to build and operate a solar or wind farm, success is all about end-to-end efficient execution, rather than generating a buzz in the market. Yes, they have recognized that thanks to advances in semiconductors and manufacturing, solar has become the cheapest form of electricity for more than half the planet; they also see that if one is going to build a large, say 200 MW solar farm in Spain or Texas or Argentina, you need to have the skills to acquire land, get right of way from the solar farm to where it can link with the grid or the customer, conclude attractive contracts for sale of the power, choose suppliers for the panels and all the balance of plant equipment that are both cost competitive and reliable, employ the workers to build safely and with quality work, and then run the thing exceptionally well so as to make good returns for the investors.

Now all of this might seem a bit boring, but it turns out that it is hard to do. If you do it well, have the processes and people to execute this, the company can do it over and over again. By assembling the team that is skilled at executing across the entire business process from conception to operation, you have created a competitive barrier that others will have difficulty replicating. The result is a good business that is unlikely to fail and will provide good returns to investors.

Failure rate can be reduced, and average returns can be improved, by having a mix of these 'boring' businesses in any portfolio.

Intellectual Property

I have mentioned protection of intellectual property as something that start-ups sometimes sacrifice because they don't have sufficient funds. It is worth some further consideration as a cause of failure. The last two centuries' history of entrepreneurship was certainly about inventions, with developing and defending a significant patent portfolio at the heart of creating a valuable and successful business. This is still the case for pharmaceuticals, for chemical processes, and for a variety of other device-related businesses. While I do not see intellectual property as among the major causes of failure these days, it is worth a discussion.

Intellectual property is more than patents. It is copyright, registered trademarks, how your brand is presented to the market through a memorable slogan or association with a celebrity, trade secrets, and just know-how. Some of this property is more intellectual than others!

It is obvious that if you are a start-up trying to bring to market a new chemical process and you have no patent protection, your chance of failure is great. It is hard, though not that hard, to reverse engineer such a process and take advantage of all the research you have done but failed to protect, though there will likely be secrets that have not been disclosed in your patents. Even with patent protection, as a start-up you will generally be facing companies with far greater resources who may infringe on your position.

The first question any start-up, or investor, needs to ask is whether someone else has intellectual property, particularly in the form of patents, copyrights or trademarks, which will prevent you from bringing the product you are proposing to market. This is called Freedom to Operate, and I have seen several start-ups where, to save money, neither the founders nor the investors paid for professional advice on whether the company had freedom to operate. The problem doesn't become apparent right at the beginning because those holding the relevant patents don't even know you exist. As a result, money is spent, work is done, you start tackling the market, only to get a letter from the attorneys representing a competitor asserting that you are infringing several of their patents, which they duly list. What often happens at this point is a panicky response, instead of a calm, professional examination. It is this panic that leads to failure, more than the existence of the problem.

The second failure mode relating to patents occurs during the early years of the company. Assuming there is freedom to operate, the start-up and its investors are keen to build a patent portfolio for the company. This can be something of value. Indeed, there are numerous examples of start-ups where getting the product into manufacture and establishing it in the market has failed, but investors recoup some or all of their money through sale of the intellectual property. How then does this become a failure mode?

Patenting is not just about writing up an application and filing it every time you think you have an invention. For a start-up, it requires an intellectual property strategy. What you want to do is imagine the area in which the company is trying to work as a map, on which you have your region to defend, then consider the patents as barriers you are trying to create – basically a moat around your business. Think about the work you have done in the lab and try to create the most broad-based patents you can write to protect the company. A qualified patent firm will help you with this. After you are successful with getting this broad-based protection, then shore it up with specific implementations. Yes, all this costs money; not doing it this way could cost you the company. The key point is that the strategic approach to intellectual property protection is money well spent, whereas starting with patenting extremely specific, somewhat random things, is money that is likely wasted. Moreover, once you have patents granted, there is more money to be spent, first to extend their coverage to broader geographies, second to maintain and defend these patents. These costs are material to an early-stage company, and need to be planned for, as they often occur ahead of significant revenue generation. This is a worthwhile expenditure when the patents are serving a strategic purpose.

Some of the cleverest companies I have seen, in hotly competitive areas, have invented things and filed patents in aspects of their technology that they are not actually bringing to market. This is also strategic, as it misleads competitors, while being completely legal. Once again, it is an expense that must be carefully considered.

There are things that a company has developed that should always be kept secret, and patents are by their very nature disclosure. However, it is a warning sign to me when founders, questioned about their intellectual property strategy, just say that everything is being kept as a trade secret. It almost always indicates a lack of understanding of the way that having a well thought out intellectual property strategy creates value for the company.

The board, representing the investors, should have as a regular agenda item: 'Review of the Company's Intellectual Property Portfolio'. The board's emphasis must be strategy and risk, and this agenda item deals with both, as well as the LTV of the company. A company that is going to fail will probably find other ways to do so, once it is clear that it has freedom to operate, but getting intellectual property right, particularly taking a strategic approach that is well funded, using professional advice, is an essential aspect of building valuation.

Intellectual property is an asset that can be valued in a quantitative way. As such, it should become part of the company's balance sheet, alongside other assets and liabilities. Ultimately, and by that I mean when a company is ready to be sold or taken public, having an outstanding intellectual property portfolio can be the difference between being sold for 5–6x its earnings and 20–30x. The lack of a portfolio of protected intellectual property at this stage might not be the source of failure, but it has the potential for being a differentiator in magnitude of success.

Avoiding the Little Traps That Bite Your Ankle

Readers of daily newsletters like Medium will know that practically every day someone writes a short piece with their list of the ten biggest reasons start-ups fail. Most of them will be a version of the six main causes I have discussed at length. I have limited myself to seven more in this section, influenced by those that have been important in my own experience.

All these little things, and most of the big ones, are about risks. As a start-up founder, you are creating a business that has risks all around you. Unfortunately, they don't appear as big flashing red lights, but simply as events. With the big risks – imperfect understanding of the market and its structure, insufficient quality and quantity of engineering, too little money for the time it takes to build a real business and so on – smart founders, company leadership, and their boards will appreciate these and steer the company through them with planning and wisdom. The smaller ones are like little traps along the path, or more likely off to the side, so you need peripheral vision to avoid them. They can be damaging, and occasionally fatal.

When Jensen Huang of Nvidia said that building a company is 'insanely difficult', I think that he meant, at least in part, that the leader must have the sort of peripheral vision and instinctual anticipation of where risks will occur, as well as a bias for action that they can use to mitigate those risks before they become life-threatening to the company.

Notes

1   J.M. Utterback, *Managing the Dynamics of Innovation*, Harvard Business School Press, 1994.

10

We Can Do This Better

Finding a Successful Path

I have tried to describe the myriad ways that start-ups fail and give a guide for actions that can be taken to avoid, or at least reduce the probability, of these modes of failure. There certainly seems to be a lot of choices that both leaders of start-up companies and investors make that can lead them to lose their money, while putting in a lot of effort. I have highlighted six big causes of failure that I know occur frequently in the start-up world, especially with technology companies, as well as seven smaller ones that happen often enough that they make some people's top ten as traps you can fall into. All this is about learning where things can go wrong, from the very beginning to later in company life. Now I want to ask, is there a way to start off on a better path, and stay on that path as the company grows and prospers? That is what I am going to consider in this section. To get on that path, indeed, to prove that such a path exists, I am going to describe both strategies and tools for investors and for entrepreneurs.

At the first stage, where the questions are 'Should we invest?' and 'Is this idea and this team one that can be successful?' it may seem that this is only of interest to the investment firm. Properly done this is not the case. If investors can ask probing questions rather than formulaic ones, they have a chance of making more intelligent decisions about investment. Even when those decisions are negative, if they then give feedback to the founders about why they decided not to invest, perhaps why they wouldn't even listen to a presentation, that is a substantive contribution to both parties. Founders receiving such responses who are smart enough to take them on board, rather than just think of comments to refute the decision, will either save themselves a lot of effort in pursuit of an idea that will fail, or take corrective actions to make their company investable. Still, this depends on the investors doing their job exceptionally well at this stage. I have commented earlier in this book about the bad results that occur when arrogance, especially from one person in a senior position of a venture fund, perverts the decision-making process. The best decisions in business are made when the contributions of everyone at the table are heard and valued. I am going to describe some techniques that I think can help investors be a lot better than average.

Once the partnership exists between founders and their investors, the challenging work begins to turn an idea into something that can be successful. This is about creating a new business, often it is about taking a small business to the next level, and everyone must recognize that this doesn't happen in a week or a month. It takes time. While much of what I have described in previous sections have been tactical issues – educating the market, getting engineering right, board alignment, leadership development – tactics are not enough. Even for a start-up, strategy is also required. There are many ways universities and short courses teach strategic thinking methodology for business.[1] I have found that most of these are designed to be used by large, established companies. An exception is Hamilton Helmer's '7 Powers' approach,[2] which I believe provides excellent focal points for strategic discussions by boards together with founders of start-ups, while working equally well for more mature companies. Because this is not as well known as I think it should be, I will give a brief, start-up-oriented, introduction to it.

Before you can march a business down the path to success you have to know where you are going, that is the strategy. To execute on the strategy – and

I have already quoted John Doerr's famous maxim, 'Ideas are easy, execution is everything' – companies need to focus on what they are going to achieve, and by when. It's not just a revenue number, or even a profit number. Those are outcomes that happen because of specific things that the company's product can accomplish, which competitors cannot do as well. Companies that get on the path to success do so because they set very specific goals, both for the company and for each individual. This works whether you are in a small company or a big one. Everyone needs to know just what they need to get done in this month, quarter or this year, and understand how that will make the company successful. For a company with a small number of employees, the leader must make this clear in discussions with everyone. In turn, this means the leader needs to have thought through why they are asking one of their precious staff to accomplish a particular goal by a certain date. As the company grows, more of this burden falls on the managers of various groups. Still, great leaders address all the employees regularly in town hall meetings or whatever format is appropriate, communicating effectively just what the company needs to get done to survive and prosper, in such a way that every employee can understand how they are contributing to that prosperity.

Yet another component of 'The Right Path' is human behaviour, particularly how we make decisions. In any start-up there are daily decision points. While some are small things, or appear to be, they are almost all consequential. I think it is important for the leadership, both management and investors, to be aware of how the framing of an issue influences how we decide what to do about it. Of still greater importance is understanding how our customers make decisions. The presentation of the product to the customer must be driven by this sort of understanding, and I don't think this happens often enough. There are some truths about our brains when it comes to decisions that are now being recognized as being universal, largely as a result of Richard Thaler, Cass Sunstein, and Daniel Kahneman's work on behavioural economics.[3] Too few start-ups, in my experience, take the time to learn about behavioural economics, let alone utilize it in their business life. This is a big subject, I can only introduce it briefly, but with the hope that readers will be sufficiently intrigued to dive deeper into it.

Finally, the right path involves designing and adapting the organization of the company to achieve difficult things while going through multiple stages of development, then leading that organization so it can accomplish extraordinary things. It is obvious that there is no one organizational model that is going to work from starting with five employees to being a company with millions in sales. What is the right approach to this?

The Right Path: Making Investment Decisions More Efficient

Getting on the path to more successful companies starts with making excellent decisions on whether to invest, then communicating both the positive and negative decisions to the companies with detailed and constructive feedback. When the answer is no, is it because we think the idea is basically flawed, or we don't believe the market is there, or your team is too weak? Some of these things are correctable, some aren't. Investors add value in how they communicate negative decisions, and it will, eventually, mean that people bring the best ideas and the best companies to them first. Even when the decision is positive, a number of concerns will have been raised if there was a good discussion among the investment professionals around the table. Those also need to be provided as feedback, because they are bound to resurface soon in the life of the company post investment.

One of the things that investors struggle with is the enormous number of start-ups approaching them for funding. Most have relatively few people who can be spending their time meeting with a founder and deciding whether this is worth the partners spending time evaluating. It is essential that firms have a way of ruling out which areas are not within their scope. Some will say, oh, many firms already do this because they are biotech investors, or cleantech, or only do software. I would counter that is not sufficient. In any of these areas you will still get 1,000 companies approaching you every year, though you will probably make, at most, ten investments. There needs to be a way to screen out those that you should not even listen to.

Here is one method that can be quite effective. First, challenge everyone in the firm (and if you have external advisers, they need to be part of this exercise) to make a list of all the areas that they might see as proposals for investment. Even if you say that we only invest in things that mitigate climate change, for example, this might run to several pages of possibilities. Once you have the list, and have eliminated duplication, then get everyone to rank each area as red – definitely would not want to invest in this; amber/yellow – might be interesting; and green – definitely we should look at ideas in this area. When you have tabulated the results, you can at least screen out those that are overwhelmingly red, and screen in those that are overwhelmingly green. Gathering the group for a discussion which mainly focuses on the yellows, or those where half the group said red and half said green, can be very educational, because if you have good partners and a good atmosphere for discussion, people will defend their ratings. The outcome of all this is a consensus that of the 1,000 approaches we get, a considerable number will be eliminated because, 'sorry, we have decided that is not an area we wish to invest in'. This is a big and necessary increase in efficiency, with a co-benefit of focus.

Focus is important here, because as soon as a biotech firm says one of the things we are definitely interested in is mRNA vaccines, everyone can become educated about the state of the art, the leaders in the field, regulatory hurdles and so on. This is time consuming, and you can't possibly do it well if you are trying to cover all of biotech. When I was doing cleantech investing we had similar deep dives on electric vehicles, biofuels and chemicals from biomass, and desalination. Could this work as well for software investment? I think it can, because you can rule in or out areas such as games, gambling, or social networking, then work to achieve the same levels of understanding, efficiency and focus.

Even if you do this, there will come a time when someone in the firm says, 'I know we said we would never invest in (for example) desalination, but you have to listen to these guys because what they have is exceptional, and I think it could be a big win for us.' Tough call, and one that I think the leader of the firm needs to listen to and, probably once a year, agree to, and even then, the decision may be no.

The Right Path: Making Investment Decisions More Effective

Now the firm is listening to founders in areas that they know are of interest. Are they listening intelligently, and are they asking good questions? If there are 10 people around the table or participating online, is the person leading the discussion ensuring that all voices are heard? Chairing a meeting where presenters are being evaluated as suitable cases for investment is a skill that requires practice, feedback (who is willing and able to give this?), and understanding of what each participant can bring to the discussion and decision. At the end of the private discussion that follows the presentation, the leader must summarize, reducing what may have taken two hours into a few key points. Because this is likely to be a partnership, the summary must not be just the view of the chair. It must incorporate the views of all the partners, in order that the overall decision is seen as one behind which there is a firm consensus.

Who is taking notes and recording this summary of the discussion, both with the founders in the room, and after they have left? This is not a routine task, nor is it something that can be best done by AI. It needs to be done with a view to giving feedback, which requires some sophistication. A good firm will have one of the other partners doing this, though the temptation is to allocate it to the most junior person at the table.

This is all about structure. What about content? Founders come in and do a presentation. If they are smart, they will boil this down to approximately 8 slides. This is as good a place as any to say what this presentation needs to include. You can find many versions of this in various places, here is one I have used as a guide for many founders:

One sentence description of the business and what it does. I know you think it is amazing, and a bit complex, and one sentence could never capture it. You still need to do this in one sentence at the beginning.

Why are you raising money, how much, for what share of the business. And what will you do with the money – help fill orders already received, build the engineering team, get first traction in a big market... Some presentations leave this to the end, but I think it is better to get it out upfront, because what follows makes the case for the ask.

The management team, why they are the ones to deliver this, highlighting relevant experience. Track record is important here, but first-time founders also get funded, so don't try to overstate. You might use this slide to indicate a significant gap that you want help in filling, because this gets the investors thinking about how they can be part of solving your problem, meaning they are already on your side.

Where did the idea come from, a little (very little) bit of history; if there is a university that has retained rights to the technology this is a good place to deal with that in a definitive way rather than making it something you are answering later. If there is already any patent protection, mention it here.

The product or service, the market and its size, and the competitors. You need to describe all these; do it concisely, without being glib or overly optimistic. The more sophistication you can bring to the discussion of the market the better.

Where are you going to make the stuff, or centre of operations, along with any concerns about supply chain and delivery.

How are you going to manage marketing and sales. Be thoughtful about this before you come into the room.

Finances. Nothing complex here, cash sales already if there are any, projections, what does it take to get to cash positive, and a quick note on who owns the company now. There will be a temptation to talk about exit strategy, I think this should only be included if this is a later stage funding round. You can expect that someone in the room is bound to ask about exit, if only because they can't think of anything more intelligent to say.

And then *summarize*, probably repeating the one sentence description and the ambition of the team to make this a big business.

All of this says that a great presentation will be concise rather than rambling, confident not aggressive or listless, ambitious while being realistic on growth and valuation. It conveys excitement and gives confidence that this has a real shot at being a 10x or better outcome for the investors.

Having heard this, the burden shifts from the founders to the potential investors. Can you figure out whether these guys know what they are talking about or have they memorized a script? If you dive one level deeper on finances, do they have answers? Hopefully there is someone in the room who can ask probing questions about the technology, because the first thing you are trying to figure out is does this actually work, followed by what resources are going to be required to get from where they are now to a commercial product.

What we don't want to hear during this precious time are a bunch of questions that are asked to make a person seem smart in front of their colleagues, or that they heard someone else ask at a previous presentation. The chair or meeting leader needs to be guiding the discussion, making sure that it covers a range of points and doesn't get stuck in one narrow area. A great chair will be looking to be sure everyone who wants to ask a question gets a chance. There may or may not be strict time constraints on the meeting – in my view it is better to take the time you need, whether that turns out to be thirty minutes or two hours, rather than cut off when there are still points to be clarified.

Now the team leaves the room, and the Chair needs to hear views from everyone, preferably starting with the less senior people and moving to the partners. Far too often in venture capital firms, the minute the door is closed the most senior partners give their opinion, and more junior people are left with nothing to say except, 'I agree'. Go around the room, get everyone's voice in, challenge people to defend their positions, then summarize and achieve consensus around a decision. It is this that will be used to provide both the decision and to feed back the key points raised to the founders.

The outcome of an effective meeting between founders and investors is thus a consensus decision, with diverse views expressed, never dominated by one person, with constructive feedback to the founders, whether the decision is to invest or not to invest. This is how investors and founders start down the right path.

Strategy and the Path to Success

It may be surprising, but until about 1960 strategy was a term mainly used in discussing military planning, rather than business. Once businesses started to think strategically, it became pervasive in everything from undergraduate business courses to boardrooms. There are many attempts to put into words what we mean by strategy in business, particularly distinguishing it from tactics and operational excellence. Michael Porter's works better than most for me. He said, strategy is a 'broad formula for how a business is going to compete, what its goals should be, and what policies will be needed to carry out those goals' and the 'combination of the *ends* (goals) for which the firm is striving and the *means* (policies) by which it is seeking to get there'.[4]

I was an academic scientist and university Dean for many years, and we rarely talked about strategy in the university. Because I worked with many leaders in industry even then, I heard lots about strategy and strategic thinking, so I decided I better learn about it. In 1980, the dominant thinking was methodology that had emerged from General Electric, with most time being spent on a so-called (SWOT) analysis, that is, look at your business in terms of Strengths, Weaknesses, Opportunities and Threats. I find that this works satisfactorily, and people still use it, however it is not well suited to start-ups.

Another business fad that became prominent in the 1990s was that strategy had to be defined in a single sentence, such as John F. Kennedy's 'Our country will send a man to the moon and bring him back again safely' or Eisenhower's approach to reconquering Europe in the Second World War 'across Africa, up Italy, and into France'. One might imagine a strategy statement like this for the early days of Facebook, 'the place where everyone with internet access, young and old, shares their experiences, thoughts, and dreams'. More usually, however, strategy, if it is going to be useful for a company in aligning staff, making decisions, and beating the competition, must be more than a sentence.

Too often start-ups think about strategy very superficially. It generally doesn't feature in their pitch to investors, or if it does, they go for the one sentence version. The founder mentality, and I'm not saying this is entirely bad, is usually, 'we have the greatest product to solve a difficult problem, meaning this is going to be a big and profitable business'. It is not bad as an attitude; it is not worth much as a strategy.

Investing in start-ups and working on their boards for many years has led me to Hamilton Helmer's *7 Powers*, which he first published in book form in 2016, and is the culmination of many decades of experience advising companies at all stages. It is the one book on strategy that, at least in part, seems to be directed to getting start-up companies on the right path. Sure, companies fail more because of poor execution than a weak or incorrect strategy. However companies that succeed, which is what we want to be talking about, have a well thought out strategy that drives execution. Moreover, as Helmer points out, the different components of strategy, the 'powers', are not of equal importance at the same time. Companies need to develop certain strategic advantages early on, which then enables them to reach a next stage where other 'powers' become important, what Helmer refers to as power progression.

It is this staged approach that works so well for start-ups and is lacking in many other formulations of business strategy. First you invent a product or process, and you see how it creates value for customers. There may be competitors, and they should respond to your invention, but they don't because they have an existing profitable business which they don't want to let go of. Once your customers have adopted your solution, it might become costly for them to switch to an alternative, even if by now your competitors have responded. As you get more customers, your costs come down, creating a further barrier to competition. At some point, if you have worked at it, your brand becomes an important source of power. This is the progression of strategic power.

I can't do justice to a 200-page book in a concise summary here. To help start-ups onto the right strategic path it is useful to look at the seven powers in the way that Helmer does, namely what is the power, how does it benefit the company that has it, and how does it create a barrier to competitors. I am being qualitative in my description of each power. If you read *7 Powers* you will find ways to assess each of these more quantitatively. Because I am focusing on start-ups, I will describe the powers in a different order from Helmer, and with different amounts of emphasis.

Cornered Resource

What does this company have right at the start that no competitor has or can acquire? There are two fairly obvious examples of cornered resource. The first is either one particular genius, or, more commonly, a small core team with complementary skills and competencies that cannot be duplicated. The second is intellectual property, usually in the form of several patents that mean anyone trying to get into the business must invent something different or find a way to work around these patents. For certain kinds of tech start-ups, knowhow and experience are a potential part of intellectual property as a cornered resource. People and intellectual property create a barrier, but there is a difference. Patents are property; people are not. People are only a cornered resource if you can retain them in the company, or they are the company – that is the founders are the resource, and they have every incentive to stay with the company.

In considering some of the types of start-ups I have been interested in over the years, there is a combination of people and intellectual property, not necessarily in the form of patents, which is a cornered resource. Many of the best technological breakthroughs are quite difficult to make in quantity, that is, achieving a high yield of reliable product. You could read the patents, you could even acquire the right to use the patent, and you still would not have the ability to make the product, because there is a lot of 'know-how' involved. A good example is proprietary catalysts used in certain chemical processes. Even with sophisticated analytical tools it is not possible to reverse engineer these by getting a sample of the working catalyst and breaking it into its components. The technical team that invented and perfected the catalyst has learned that you first have to dope it with a few parts per million of element X, then bake it at Y degrees for 45 minutes, and then add a few parts per million of element Z. Those attempting to replicate the catalyst can see the presence of X and Z, but only in their final forms. The same can be true with various electro-optical devices. You can buy all the chips for such a device, even understand the wiring diagram, without knowing how they are aligned, how various levels and biases are set, all of which is pretty much impossible to figure out without the key experts.

A cornered resource in the form of people and intellectual property, especially the combination of these two, leading to a product that can provide a superior solution to an important problem, allows a company to charge more for its product, providing the potential to be a highly profitable business. Understanding this as a foundation of strategy for a start-up will mean that a board and company leadership make choices about how they prioritize growth and retention of the cornered resource.

Counter-Positioning

Many start-ups are trying to enter a business where there is already a strong incumbent. This is quite different, strategically and tactically, from solving a problem where there is no solution today. Technology may be disruptive in both situations. How you beat a strong incumbent requires considerable strategic thinking about how that incumbent will react. The key starting point for counter-positioning is that the solution offered by the start-up has to be easily substituted for the one offered by the incumbent.

As Helmer describes this, the incumbent competitor has a good, perhaps longstanding, profitable business. These incumbents look at the new technology and must ask themselves some key questions. Let's assume that the start-up challenger does not have a cornered resource as just described. The incumbent can respond to the technological challenge to their business and move to adopt the novel approach to solving the customer's problem. In doing so, they are not necessarily gaining anything. All they are doing is switching their existing customer from product A to product B. They are cannibalizing their business.

Such an incumbent must ask themselves a number of questions: We know what we bring to our existing product (in terms of technology, scale, brand, etc.). What would we bring to the new approach? Helmer discusses Kodak's response to digital photography in these terms (which may or may not have been an example of counter-positioning on the part of those offering digital photography), and I would raise the current case of oil companies getting into investing in solar energy or electric vehicle charging to offset loss of sales in their core product. They can certainly do it, but other than capital, what do they bring to the party?

The incumbents might also ask, 'We must invest to change. Will that investment produce greater returns than just milking the existing business? Sure, it might be an endgame, but endgames can be quite profitable, as we can stop investing in the next generation of our product.'

The answers that the incumbent reaches can be extremely beneficial to the start-up. Strategically, they are adopting a position against a powerful player who, correctly or incorrectly, chooses not to respond. Effectively, this is counter-positioning.

Clearly, there is disruptive technology that is not counter-positioning, and Helmer discusses a few cases of this. There can certainly be cases where there are numerous incumbents and they respond in diverse ways, making counter-positioning an ineffective strategy. An example might be the ATM machine, which was certainly disruptive if your business was running bank branches staffed from 9 am to 3 pm, and where there were numerous incumbents. Which ones reacted differently?

Counter-positioning is about more than technology challenges to solving a problem. It is often about business models. In the start-up world we probably focus too much on disruptive technology and too little on disruptive business models. Challenging an incumbent through the mechanism by which the solution to their problem is delivered (effectively the business model) can be more powerful than the technology. Many companies are so deeply committed to their way of doing business with their customers that it is written on the walls of their offices, in their advertisements and on their websites. They should be able to change, but they just can't bring themselves to do it. The start-up that realizes this has a strong strategic advantage that they can exploit.

The board and leadership of every start-up in an industry with an incumbent or several powerful incumbents needs to be asking, from day one, how will these guys react when they find out about us? Will they try to buy us (possibly a good outcome), will they find a way to kill us (certainly a bad outcome), or will they just say, well, we have a good business so good luck to these upstarts, it's not our problem. Sometimes being a quiet rather than a brash challenger leads to a better outcome for the start-up. Understanding this or at least making some informed guesses and then being vigilant in watching what happens, can lead to counter-positioning as a strategic advantage.

Scale Economies

It is the rare start-up that is profitable, even cash positive, in its early days. If it is, this is usually because it is a small business that is intending to remain small. Companies raise money in the early days because they need to invest to grow, and that investment must require larger amounts than they can self-generate.

Likewise, when you are making a small quantity of a product, costs are going to be higher, significantly higher, than you would expect them to be when you have managed to achieve industrial scale. There are two key strategic questions that must be answered up front for any product-based company:

> Is there a price point, when we are producing at a reasonable scale, that we can charge our customers such that we can make a profit?

> At the price that we believe our customers will want to pay for our product, are we competitively advantaged over other solutions to the customer's problem that we are solving?

As I have pointed out earlier, the answer to the first question needs to be based on facts rather than supposition. It is not enough to say, well, as we scale up our costs will come down. The leadership of the company needs to look at each component of cost and try to quantify where cost reductions will occur. It is very much a bottom-up analysis of the components of cost reduction rather than a top-down assertion. Regarding the second question, you can never assume that your competitor will stand still. If they already have scale, and are making a profit, they may choose to cut costs just to squeeze you.

To achieve scale economies as a strategic power you need both a benefit and a barrier. For a start-up, the key thing is getting to scale. In many cases start-ups are competing against other start-ups trying to solve the same problem by similar or quite different technological approaches. Getting to scale first gives you benefits in terms of purchasing power and pricing power that your competitor start-ups don't have. In effect, you are then both a start-up and an incumbent. Your strategic mentality has to shift to reflect your advantaged position.

Geography is also a factor in scale economy. If your customer base is concentrated geographically, expansions within that geography can often be done at advantaged economics compared to competitors who are spread over a larger area. The infrastructure that you need to support the product, as well as marketing costs, for example, will not grow as fast as your sales. Hence, scale economy. Now the barrier is your pricing power, because as you grow, if you are profitable, you can sacrifice increased margin for still greater scale, causing yet more pain for your competitor.

It will not be easy for the board and management of a start-up to make projections of economics from few units with a few customers, but this still needs to be part of every board strategy discussion. It informs the pace at which growth needs to occur, or, conversely, how much fundraising needs to be done before the company is self-sustaining. Decisions on planned market expansion will be informed by this understanding. It is also a key element of guessing what the competitive landscape is going to be. Critically done, it may say, right at the start, that unless we can find a way to do something radically different, our wonderful technology is never going to be profitable. That might not mean giving up. It could say this is what our Research and Development team needs to achieve, and by when, if we are going to survive.

Switching Costs

When start-ups think about pricing strategy to displace an incumbent, they look at the numbers. We believe that the competitor is charging customers $20,000 for this software package, plus $2/user/month. We can supply a better solution for an upfront cost of $12,000 and still make a good margin. Customers will abandon the competitor's product and flock to us.

Yet it doesn't happen. Why? Because there is a cost in switching from one software product to another. Some of this cost is real and quantifiable. We have to budget three weeks in which our systems may be partially or completely down. Or we have to invest $50,000 in training all our employees on the new package. When there is hardware involved in the new solution that a start-up is offering, customers just look at the simple payback time. Sure, this is going to work better, and we will reduce waste in our process, but how long does it take for that reduced waste to compensate for the cost of switching to the new valve? Six months, let's try it. Four years, well, no one will thank me for making that decision.

Sometimes switching costs are a bit softer. The supplier of the incumbent product has in place technical support people, who are helpful to the customer, always on the other end of the phone in case of a problem. Why give this up?

A start-up trying to displace an incumbent must consider more than just competitive pricing in understanding whether customers will abandon their current product. That is the negative aspect of strategic thinking. Now let's turn it around and look at switching costs positively. How do start-ups embed switching costs for their customers?

I have mentioned the formidable company Math Works. It adopted a strategy from the outset of selling its product, MATLAB, at a low cost to universities educating engineers, perhaps 10 per cent of what it would charge an industrial user. Today it is used in more than 5,000 colleges and universities globally. The result was, and is, that it is likely that every new engineering hire is trained on this software. If a company doing engineering design wants to use a competitor's product they have to retrain their engineers on new software. Math Works has built in switching costs into its pricing and roll out strategy, and this switching cost advantage has been maintained for four decades.

One of the key metrics all start-ups use is the ratio of the long-term or lifetime value of the customer to the company to their customer acquisition cost: LTV/CAC. This is what needs to be maximized. I raise this in the discussion of switching costs, because in addition to being a barrier to losing a customer, there is a benefit in that your company can sell customers other products that build on the first core solution. You have a customer that, once acquired, sticks with you, providing ongoing LTV, where you don't drive LTV with price increases (indeed you might even lower the price for loyal customers) but with additional products and features. By exploiting this benefit, there is a virtuous circle where you increase the barrier for competitors, that is, your product features have increased the customer's switching costs.

Start-ups, in their strategic thinking, probably need to focus on the switching costs barrier they are facing from incumbents, trying to understand this through customer conversations and quantitative marketing studies. However, once you have some success in the market, the strategic conversation turns to how can I make switching costs a benefit to my company, and a barrier to others.

Network Economies

Network Economies is a quite simple idea, which, in contrast to the strategic powers I have discussed already, is more specific – that is, it applies to certain types of products and not to others. At heart it is quite easy to understand yet can be exceedingly difficult to achieve. Everyone reading this book has lived through the rise of social media such as Facebook, LinkedIn, and Twitter. They are perfect exemplars of network economies. LinkedIn with 1,000 users scattered across geography and industries is of little value. Once it has 100 million users it is a behemoth, because everyone needs to be on it. When a company today starts recruiting for a senior executive or non-executive board member, the first thing they or their head-hunter does is look at the candidates' LinkedIn profile. I stopped carrying business cards more than five years ago because people who meet me at conferences or dinners simply look up my name on LinkedIn and make contact through it.

While the idea is clear, there can be a blurry boundary in the distinction between scale economies and network economies. Or perhaps some businesses have both. When a business achieves density in a service it is offering within a particular geographic area, for example a city, it has clear scale economies – the infrastructure to run that business at scale is cheaper than for a competitor entering the same geography with few customers. At the same time, the density of users can form a network, that customers and the business both see as a powerful advantage.

The value of the company in an example such as LinkedIn comes from the size of the network, and the competitive barrier is how difficult it is to build anything of comparable scale. This strategic power is distinct from scale economies, already discussed, because it explicitly involves the value that each customer perceives from the fact that there are so many other customers using the same product.

Uber can be thought of as another example of network economy, though less clearly distinct from scale economy. From the point of view of the customer who needs to get home after a late night out or get to a meeting across town for which they are already late, they want a car, and they want it fast. They don't care who the driver is providing the solution to their problem; they like to see the network of drivers in their vicinity one of whom will be there in two minutes. The drivers don't care who their customer is, though they prefer those that give generous tips, they just want the network to operate efficiently to minimize their time without a fare paying passenger in their car. From the business point of view, both the drivers and the customers benefit from the network and stay loyal to it as long as it is the superior solution to meeting both of their needs.

The graveyard of start-up failures is littered with challengers who either did not appreciate the value of network economies, or the barrier to penetrating a market whose profitability relies on this particular power. Founders and boards need to be clear thinking from the outset about whether this is a major or minor factor for their companies, setting their strategy accordingly.

Branding

We all know the famous brands, whether in luxury goods (Louis Vuitton, Tiffany, Hermes), soft drinks (Coke, Pepsi) or hotels (Hilton, Ritz Carlton, Four Seasons). These brands were established in the mind of customers over exceptionally long periods of time. They stand for something – quality, value, prestige – sometimes maintained over generations. As a result, the products associated with these brands command a higher price than those of their competitors, hence superior margins.

Brands are not only associated with luxury, of course. Walmart and Costco are also established brands that stand for something different – even if you are not rich, you will get an excellent product here at a lower price than elsewhere.

What these have in common is that it took a long time to get these perceptions embedded in the minds of large numbers of customers. Still, we have seen brands established relatively quickly, for example Airbnb. What we don't know yet is the durability of the brand.

Just as with intellectual property, it is possible to do some quantification of how much a brand is worth, and to include that on the company's balance sheet. This contrasts with some of the other strategic powers I have already described, which rarely feature explicitly on corporate balance sheets.

Brand development as a strategic power is not something that is universal, or that every company must strive for. Recall how important it is for start-ups to figure out the structure of the markets they are trying to access – how does new technology get adopted by the established big players? Sometimes this means that you will be successful by having one of the Tier 2 suppliers take up your product, repackage it under their brand, and sell it. You might wish you had visibility, but you should be thankful you have a good sales pipeline, with someone else doing the selling for you. In this situation, strategic thinking says don't waste time and resources trying to build brand. The notable example of this is TSMC, Taiwan Semiconductor Manufacturing Company. Its products are in virtually all semiconductor devices, yet its name never appears. You might think this is an exception, but it is a big one and representative of quite a lot of technology successes.

Start-ups sometimes fall into the trap of thinking that brand is all about image. After all, we can recognize a Coca-Cola or Starbucks even without reading the name. Start-ups then spend a lot of time designing and perfecting their logo, changing the colour, tagline, font, asking people what they think and redoing it endless times. Great branding is not about this. It is about establishing customer trust and loyalty because they love your product. Having a great logo doesn't get you customers. Good market intelligence and persistence at sales is what you need to do first. When the first hundred customers tell you that they now love your product (even if they didn't at first) and they will trust you enough that they buy more of the same or your next product, then you are on the way to building a brand. A great logo or tagline reinforces this, makes it easy for customers to recognize the product when they see it, but it is only of value when it is backed by customer trust.[5]

Brands are an important part of the value of many successful corporations. There is considerable skill required to build one, and to maintain it. Start-ups and their leadership that see branding as a crucial part of their LTV should be sure they have the expertise to capture that value.

Process Power

The final one of Helmer's *7 Powers* is Process Power. It is formidable, when you have it, because it is notoriously hard to replicate. I would describe it as related to the culture of a company that enables it to produce superior product, quickly, and at lowest cost. A phrase that probably captures it for companies is 'the way we do things around here'.

Process power is distinguishable from pure operational excellence in execution of, for example, manufacturing, or software updates. One might think that companies producing the very same product, for example automobiles, or fuels for vehicles, would have converged on a way of doing this, after a century or so of experience, meaning that there would be little difference between them in how they deliver the product. As it turns out, this is not the case. Why?

Because companies are made up of people, not just machines. There are companies that use very rigid procedures and are highly centralized in declaring how things will be done. Others allow units operating in various parts of the world, or distinct parts of the business, to find their own way of doing things. This is corporate culture. Neither of these is 'right', if they deliver a superior result.

Still, many companies never develop this strong corporate culture that makes their employees more effective at delivering products. What is missing in such companies? When the workers at all levels can say 'look, there is a better way of doing this', and there is a process in place to allow such suggestions to be looked at, examined, and change effected, companies have a way of evolving to become better and better at delivery.

There is something about this process power that can be built at the early stage of a company's life, and it probably goes back to the leadership qualities of the founders. Do they value people or are they just arrogant about their own abilities and ideas? As the size of the workforce increases, do people see the way things are done, then both fit in and feel empowered to suggest change? For me this is how process power is built.

I have put this last in the *7 Powers* because I think it is probably the one start-ups and their boards should spend the least time on in their strategic thinking. Nonetheless, it is something to be conscious of, particularly if you can identify it, and this is not easy, as a source of competitive advantage for an incumbent you are trying to disrupt. Because it is very much a human factored power, it leads me well into the next part of my discussion about human behaviours and how we use our understanding of them to get on a successful path.

Power Progression

Every company is different; hence every strategy is distinct, and hopefully also distinctive. If your strategy was something that ChatGPT could just create for you it is unlikely to be adding much value, as your competitors would get exactly the same strategy. Most companies in the space we are considering in this book start with an idea, an invention, driven by a need that may or may not be perceived by their potential customer. Building a business is, in part, about developing a strategy to achieve dominance with that invention in the marketplace.

The strategy that a start-up company develops is about how to get a series of benefits that are not readily available to others, while creating barriers to competitors trying to eat your lunch. Development of strategy is, I think, the role of the company's board, which includes the founders and senior executives. Indeed, when executives are participating in a board meeting, they should be putting aside their thoughts and goals as managers, to think about and contribute to corporate strategy and risk.

Going back to the *7 Powers*, most companies will start by working on cornered resource, understanding what they have that others don't have and can't get. In parallel to this, they should be looking at counter-positioning, because it is the way to gain insight as to how both customers and competitors are going to react to your intrusion into their space.

As the company begins to grow, scale economies, possibly network economies, and switching costs become more important. However, these need to be part of the early strategic discussion. We recognize that technology start-ups cannot usually make money in their early life, and that is fine. What they need to convince themselves of is that there is a possibility, indeed a near certainty, that at scale they can be selling a product at a real profit, keeping in mind realistic costs. Strategic thinking at this early stage gives company leadership guideposts as to when they need to execute on creation of these three powers.

Usually, it is when a company has reached scale in the market, even though it might still have orders of magnitude of growth ahead of it, that it needs to develop the powers around branding and process power. Regarding branding, there will be clear understanding of what makes sense in terms of the company's investment in brand development. Process power, by contrast, evolves and builds over time. A wise and effective board will do enough 'walking around' among the employees to learn whether process power is being built. To learn this, they need to be conscious of its importance.

Start-ups too often focus solely on execution and do not allow time and space for developing a strategy. Helmer's *7 Powers* give us a way of doing progressive strategy development which will pay off in both the short and the long term.

People Making Decisions: Behavioural Economics for Start-Ups

More than thirty years ago, the great planner and corporate strategist Arie de Geus spoke to the Royal Society of Arts on the topic 'Companies: What are They?'[6] There is a great deal of wisdom in this article, and I recommend it highly to anyone thinking about companies. One anecdote stuck with me. When he was a student at Erasmus University in Rotterdam, they were taught:

> The production of goods and services takes place in organizations which in our societies are called companies. They produce goods for which other people are prepared to pay a price. Companies produce these goods by trying to find the optimum combination of three production factors: labour, capital and land. These three are substitutable, for example, labour can be replaced by capital. The optimum combination of production factors is the one at which the company is producing at minimum costs to be sold at maximum price for the maximization of profits.

De Geus says that,

> To us students, it was a reassuring definition. It made a company into a rational entity ... It sounded so controllable: if you have trouble with labour or if it is too expensive, you replace manpower by capital assets. For young aspiring corporate leaders ... this description of their future place of work was reassuring and comforting: rational, calculable, and controllable.

When he went on to his first job at Shell's Rotterdam refinery, 'a feeling of discomfort developed quickly. The theories (we had been taught) mentioned labour but there was no talk of people. Yet the real world . . . seemed to be full of them. And because the workplace was full of people, it looked suspiciously as if companies were *not* always rational, calculable, and controllable.' There were all the principles and equations he had been taught, but the people working in the refinery didn't know that they were supposed to be making their decisions according to principles taught at Erasmus, so they just went about their jobs. That's one of the reasons business is difficult.

Kahneman's book *Thinking Fast and Slow* is about people and how they make decisions. It asserts and then tries to prove through discussion of a lot of experimental data, that our minds operate using two separate and distinct systems. System 1 is fast, automatic and intuitive. We use System 1 almost all the time, as we make the thousands of tiny decisions we are confronted with every day. Emotion is also part of System 1 decisions. If you think about yourself getting up in the morning, brushing your teeth, choosing what to wear, deciding on makeup, having breakfast, walking to the station, heading into your office, you have made decisions one after the other, and you have to make them quickly, or you would never get out of your bedroom.

However, there is another brain architecture for decision-making which he calls System 2. These decisions are slow, logical, deliberate and take a lot of effort. When we want to learn something new, we focus on it, work hard until we can do it right, and derive satisfaction from the learning. Sometimes the thing we have learned (for example, how to ride a bicycle) now becomes automatic, and moves from a System 2 to a system 1 activity. For me, as a manager or board member, there are many difficult things I have learned to do via System 2 thinking. Examples would be how to achieve compromise and alignment in a group of diverse individuals; how to give feedback to the CEO as Chair of the board so that it improves their relationship and strengthens it; knowing when to push harder and when to trust others to do the pushing. These are not easy, mostly (referring to our discussion on Leadership) it is because they are competencies rather than skills, and I think that they remain System 2 rather than System 1. On the other hand, listening skills, which enable a lot of these competencies to be practiced effectively, can transfer from System 2 to System 1. Likewise, the ability, in chairing a meeting, to decide what are the main points made and conclusions drawn from a discussion, summarize, and move on to the next item, all of which relies on the sophistication of our listening skills, can become an important System 1 accomplishment. Knowing the difference, in your role in a company, whether as founder or board member, is what it means to practice conscious leadership.

Thaler and Sunstein's work builds on Kahneman in helping us understand how people make decisions when they have a choice, or choices. How these choices are set out for us, often intentionally, they call choice architecture. It may involve such things as product placement in a supermarket or airport bookshop, advertising, decisions to offer you two choices even though there are five distinct products that might meet your needs.

Given this choice architecture, we are being 'nudged' towards choosing one thing or behaviour over another. Now you might argue, I am a rational human being, I don't make important economic decisions on that basis. Well, this work on behavioural economics says otherwise. We are all susceptible to being nudged towards a choice, and we don't always make our decisions based on rational economic arguments. Part of this is the effort involved. The rational choice probably requires System 2 thinking, the one that abandons rational analysis can be done by System 1.

Most of the readers of this book will have learned how to do a discounted cash flow or net present value analysis of a business decision. It is the rational way to make a choice, whether to buy product A or product B or do nothing. We rarely if ever do this when making economic decisions in our personal life, even though those can be quite consequential. In business, we do them more often, yet we are still subject to arguments like simple payback, buy this product and it will pay back your outlay in three and a half years, which discards all the rational net present value analysis methodology we have been taught. Companies trying to sell us things have learned that we can be nudged towards a decision in their favour by the simple payback argument. In effect, we have been nudged from using System 2 to using System 1.

Thinking about the strategic powers described in the previous section, quite a lot of them involve decisions a company, especially a start-up, needs to make vis a vis its competitors, and guessing how competitors are going to respond to your presence in their market. Behavioural economics as taught by Kahneman and Thaler and Sunstein gives us quite a lot of insight into how to make these decisions.

This idea of nudging potential customers to decide to try our product is what every start-up is attempting. Nudging, a subtle approach to influencing behaviour, can be a valuable tool for you when seeking to improve user engagement, conversion rates and overall product adoption. By understanding how people make decisions, you can create subtle and not so subtle design features that gently guide users towards desired outcomes without restricting their freedom of choice.

Some examples of nudging and the benefits it conveys are as follows.

Increased User Engagement

Nudges can help capture and maintain user attention, making the product more engaging and compelling. When you try a new product for the first time and it is easy to find your way in, maybe because of one or two little things that have been built into the first time user experience, the product has captivated you. Just how the start-up uses its limited resources in educating the market, and its first customers, to take notice of it makes this nudge effective or not.

Improved Conversion Rates

By subtly influencing decision-making, nudges can increase the likelihood of users taking desired actions, like signing up for a free trial or making an initial purchase without the long-term commitment that will eventually be required. Trials are important at every level, from small household products to large systems for environmental monitoring. A key decision for start-ups is whether the trial is free or paid for. In most cases, you start offering it as free, because behavioural economics has taught that everyone loves something that is 'free', and then move on to paid trials, which can also be an effective nudge if you can convince potential customers that you have many companies asking for trials and need to choose which will be given priority.

Enhanced Product Feature Adoption

Nudges can help users discover and adopt new features, ultimately leading to greater product usage and satisfaction. Initial CACs are always high. We need to use nudging of our customers to retain their loyalty and increase the lifetime value of them to us. Offering added features does just this.

Personalized User Experiences

Nudges can be tailored to individual user preferences and behaviours, creating a more personalized and engaging experience. Through understanding how our customers use our software or systems, start-ups can learn what features they value, perhaps enabling them to make choices that take a standard system with numerous features and choose the ones that are important to them. Effectively, everyone has the same product, but they use it in different ways.

Strategic thinking points us to the sorts of nudges that will be effective in building a start-up business. Or, put the other way, behavioural economics is what helps us operationalize the strategic powers we are trying to build. The following are some of the ways we can do this.

Showcasing Product Benefits

Highlighting the benefits of a product or service in a clear and concise way can nudge users towards making a purchase. Too often start-ups haven't done the work to know what benefits or services are important to a customer. When they have done it, they need to be sure that those benefits are not lost in a morass of information that is lower down on the decision-making path. I have seen start-ups begin with a good three page brochure, or two minute video. As they develop the product and get more data, they just add more and more detail, so the brochure becomes ten pages, and the benefits that will nudge the potential customer to make a buying decision are obscured.

Creating a Sense of Urgency

One method that is common is using countdown timers or limited time offers that can encourage users to act quickly. This isn't very subtle and can backfire. In my view it is more of a push than a nudge, and customers don't like to be pushed. Where there is limited availability, whether of products or people, saying this in a way that conveys honesty will nudge customers towards a decision.

Providing Social Proof

Displaying testimonials, reviews, or ratings can help build trust and influence users' decisions. Such testimonials are a way that we use to shift a decision requiring System 2 to something that is more System 1. If I accept the view that a competitor in my industry, who I respect, uses your product, that is an important validation. I don't have to do the analysis myself.

Simplifying End-to-End User Experience

Removing unnecessary steps or barriers in the user journey can make it easier for users to complete desired actions. Much of the success of our conversion to online shopping has happened because it is just simpler to fulfil a need. In turn, customer expectations have increased. As a result, next day delivery is no longer unusual. When supplying complex industrial products, start-ups need to think about how they will make cross border shipping and delivery their problem, not their customer's. In our earlier discussion about selling industrial products via Tier 1 and Tier 2 suppliers, securing this cross-border capability is one of the benefits that a start-up could never afford on its own.

Using Visual Cues

Employing clear visuals, icons, or animations can guide users through the user interface and highlight essential information. People are used to learning things now through watching videos, and start-ups should take advantage of this, rather than defaulting to an old fashioned printed manual. Linking back to our earlier point about personalized user experience, as we teach someone how to use our product, we can learn what is important to them and show them how they can tailor it to their needs. In a great start-up, the person who does this will feed back to those in charge of product development, creating a virtuous circle of improvement.

All of this can work to make our sales more effective, and our competitive position stronger. There are a few final considerations worth mentioning.

Being Ethical

It's important to use nudges responsibly and avoid manipulative tactics that could deceive or mislead users. I have mentioned ethical and unethical behaviour several times in this book. Nudges are a place where the temptation to push emotional or economic buttons through providing false or dubious information/validation is great. Don't do it. You will be found out and will destroy company value as well as your own reputation.

Understanding User Motivations

Start-ups need to understand their target audience's needs and motivations to effectively design nudges that resonate with them. Once again, we come back to the role of marketing, not just sales. Too often what passes for start-up marketing is focused completely on what the customer needs, because that is why we started the business. We saw a need, we provided a solution, so buy our product to solve your problem. Motivation is different; it can be much more diverse and less obvious. A great marketing effort learns about motivations and then uses these to do sales more effectively.

Testing and Iteration

Start-ups should test different nudges and iterate on their designs to ensure they are achieving the desired results. Well, I would say that, because I am by training a scientist, meaning I like to do experiments. I believe that one of the most important things we can do in any business is to try something, see if it works, decide if that is the exception or we have uncovered something important, learn, refine and do more experiments.

By thoughtfully incorporating principles of behavioural economics into product design, marketing, sales and user experience, start-ups can create a more engaging, efficient and ultimately successful product. Have I at least nudged you into learning more about this?

People and Structure

I have dwelt on the role of behavioural economics in getting product acceptance and making sales. Let's bring it back to the problem de Geus identified in how the individuals in the company decide what to do. Great leaders are adept at using behavioural economics to motivate employees towards exceptional performance, and to align an organization to achieve challenging goals. Recall the leadership competencies discussed earlier – builds best teams, ensures alignment, leads change, shapes performance; now we can see them through the lens of understanding how people make decisions, and how we nudge them to make better decisions for the good of the company.

Leaders need to step back regularly, by which I mean sit in their chair with the lights out and think about the day they just had, figure out what different outcomes they need to achieve, and how to nudge people towards those outcomes. Questions that arise are often about collaboration between different individuals or groups, how to structure team meetings to increase participation, even how does the leader manage their own time better.

It is often easier to identify the problem you are trying to solve than to figure out how to make change happen. That's why 'leads change' is such an important leadership competency. For me the key thing is to recognize that there are many different motivators. After spending the early part of my career as an academic, one of the things that struck me on joining a big company at management level was over-reliance on money as the single thing that motivated exceptional employee performance. By contrast, in the university it is almost completely missing as a motivational tool. Both extremes seemed wrong, and that is true in start-ups as well. People want tangible rewards for their work; in start-ups they want the promise of large tangible rewards down the line if the company is successful. Still, it is not the only thing. All sorts of public recognition, from the most subtle remark in a team meeting to formally highlighting what someone has accomplished, will motivate that person and others to try even harder. When in doubt, more recognition is usually the right choice. For a highly competent leader, a 1:1 meeting will draw out what will lead to a key staff member making an exceptional effort, and use nudges to reinforce the prospect of that recognition happening.

People in the workplace make choices on how they spend their time. Behavioural economics says that if you want them to make the right choices for the company those have to be the ones that are easy to make. This includes finding ways to make collaboration easier, for example in how objectives are agreed, or where people sit in the workplace.

As with many of the other things in this book, leaders try nudging in a particular way, that is, they do an experiment, see if it works, and then refine the nudges to increase their impact. All of this presupposes an organization in which this is happening.

Most start-ups begin without any sort of organizational structure. There are very few people, they are trying to turn an idea into a product, and they don't have a lot of money. Once there is some money, there are likely to be a few more people, all of whom need to turn their hands and minds to whatever this week's priority might be.

Now what happens when there is a substantial funding round, and the start-up needs to get on with doing all the things I have described earlier to avoid failure and get on a successful path? For sure, work becomes more specialized; some people are working on market development, others on engineering. This looks like a point where there needs to be a more formal structure put in place so that every person in the company, even if there are only a total of twenty-five of them, knows who their boss is, and who can decide what.

When John D. Rockefeller started Standard Oil, he looked for a model of how to organize the business. Now this was more than 150 years ago, and the job of management consultant had not yet been invented. Rockefeller saw only two well-functioning organizational models – the army and the Catholic Church. In each case there was a clear hierarchy, and, at least externally, it appeared that promotion was based on the upper levels evaluating those below and making decisions to promote or exit based on merit, that is to say, on how well individuals accomplished the goals of the organization. All of this aligned with his values, and it became the dominant model used by businesses large and small.

We need to ask, does this model make any sense for a technology start-up? The essential feature of the model is not that it is a meritocracy. That could be accomplished without it, indeed in almost any organization that is going to be successful the best people will find that they have more influence over what the company does, and the least competent people will leave. No, the essential feature of the model is hierarchy. The CEO has three to five people who report to them, and those people have a similar span of control. Probably the CEO and their four direct reports form a sort of executive committee, which makes decisions and informs those lower down what they have decided.

Founders, and boards, need to challenge this model. Jensen Huang, the CEO of Nvidia, has forty people who report directly to him. When he has meetings to discuss a particular problem or goal that the company needs to solve or achieve, everyone who is relevant to that is in the room, from the most senior to the most junior engineers. Start-ups have a lot to gain by having very flat organizations, as few levels as possible. Ideally, I would recommend that the number of levels should be one fewer than you think possible as you begin to organize. As the organization grows, more people being added, it is not always necessary to continue adding layers. Moreover, not every senior person in a technology start-up needs to have other people working for them. There are important roles in these companies for people who work by influence rather than by the size of their group. This only works if the CEO, CTO, and others are smart enough to listen to the smartest people in the company, hearing from them what is not working as well as it should, what can be done to make a step change in the product, and what is going on in the world outside the company that can offer opportunity or pose a threat.

Getting on the successful path is, in part, getting the organization right. We are trying to get everyone in the company to be fully committed, personally and professionally, to its success. To accomplish this they have to feel part of decisions, hear the debate and the rationale for what was concluded from that debate, and when they believe they have something to contribute know that they will be listened to respectfully, independent of seniority.

One final thing to say about how a company is organized. Whatever you choose to do, it should not be regarded as permanent. Companies change, and how the various functions are led and interact can change as well. There is no right answer, there is only the answer that is most efficacious for your company at whatever stage it is at.

A Path to Success

Many years ago, the great business guru Peter Drucker talked about how companies need to be doing the right things and doing the thing right.[7] Some people have, I think, interpreted this as requiring efficiency and effectiveness, or as the need to bring certain values to business decisions.

In the context of looking at why start-ups fail, doing the thing right is about understanding the causes of failure, both the big ones and the smaller ones, working as a team of management and board to ensure that we don't make the mistakes that are avoidable through effective funding, planning and execution, with the best people we can attract and motivate.

Doing the right thing goes beyond this. It says that to get on a successful path for building a large, viable business we need to think strategically right from the beginning, that is to say, strategy is not a luxury that only big established companies can afford. Strategic thinking will give us insights into why we will be more successful than our competitors, then we operationalize this by doing the thing right. We use strategy to define what a successful path is; we execute to stay on that path.

Doing the right thing is also about learning. AI notwithstanding, a successful start-up business is now, and will be for the foreseeable future, about people making decisions on whether to use our product to solve a problem, even if it is a problem they did not yet know they had. Behavioural economics helps us to learn how people make these decisions, meaning we can take steps to get them to choose to buy from us. Company leadership doesn't have to read a lot of books or take courses about this, but they do need to use the understanding that has developed over the last few decades to make themselves more effective.

Successful companies will always be doing the right thing for their people. In every company, especially in small companies, that means that everyone is able to contribute to discussions leading to decisions about what the company is going to do next and do it better. Companies are not democracies; after discussion the leader must make a decision, and everyone needs to do their part to implement that decision. People will do that with greater commitment and enthusiasm when their voice has been heard. Sometimes, doing the right thing for an employee is asking them to leave the company, and there can be many reasons for this. When companies are on a successful path even these tough decisions are recognized by the group as the right thing for keeping the company on that path.

One final thing. The most important thing we have as scientists, engineers, financial people, investors in start-ups are our reputations for integrity. Working in a start-up, growing it into a business that serves customers, is exceedingly difficult and comes with a lot of pressure from all sides. The simple way of looking at it is that you have cash, you are spending it at a furious rate, and unless you get traction in the market by a certain date there will be no more cash, no more company. The leadership, CEO, CFO, and others feel responsibility to their employees, their investors, their families too. It can happen that despite your best efforts you will fail. In the face of all these pressures you must never compromise on presenting data and results, both technical and financial, with scrupulous honesty.

There isn't a successful path for every company. Perhaps that becomes clear when leadership in the company asks the difficult questions that are designed to find that path, only to recognize that it doesn't exist, or at least they are not able to discern it. That is a good outcome, arrived at through thinking and using the collective wisdom of the management and the board. More often, I believe, such a path does exist, and it is worth the effort to get on it.

Notes

1. For a leading text on this, see D. Mackay, M. Arevuo and M. Meadows, *Strategy: Theory, Practice, Implementation*, 2nd edn (Oxford: Oxford University Press, 2023), which does contain a lot of advice that works for start-ups.

2. Hamilton Helmer, *7 Powers* (Los Altos, CA: Deep Strategy, 2016). I learned about this from listening to the podcasts called *Acquired*, which often discuss companies in terms of the 7 Powers, and which also have featured interviews with Hamilton Helmer.

3. R. Thaler and C. R. Sunstein, *Nudge: Improving Decisions about Health, Wealth, and Happiness* (New Haven, CT: Yale University Press, 2008); and Daniel Kahneman, *Thinking Fast and Slow* (New York, NY: Farrar, Strauss and Giroux, 2011).

4. Michael E. Porter, *Competitive Strategy* (New York, NY: Free Press, 1980).

5. I am indebted to Aaron Dinin for pointing this out so succinctly in an article, 'The Only Way to Create Loyal Customers', https//ehandbook.com/the-only-way-to-create-loyal-customers-0ea5ecd4d947, accessed 5 September 2025.

6. Arie de Geus, 'Companies: What are They?', *RSA Journal*, 143, no. 5460 (June 1995): 26–35. The observations in this article led to de Geus' idea of a living company, which were published as 'The Living Company', *Harvard Business Review*, 75, no. 2 (March–April 1997), https://hbr.org/1997/03/the-living-company, accessed 24 May 2025. In it he explores why there is such a great disparity between the longest lived companies and those that fail early.

7. His original statement was, 'Management is doing things right; leadership is doing the right things.' For more of his wisdom, see Peter Drucker, *The Essential Drucker* (London: Routledge, 2001).

11

Could This Actually Work?

I believe that everyone in the start-up world should have an ambition – to reduce the ridiculously high percentage of technology-related start-ups that fail. Failure for the entrepreneur means that you have spent precious years of your life working hard, extremely hard usually, on something about which you were passionate but for which you were never rewarded. Perhaps you learned a lot from the failure, which is good. Does that learning reduce the chance that if you did it again your probability of success would go up? You could have spent those years working for a big company, still hard but probably at much lower risk, where you would also have learned things. Failure for the investors means that there were some standard products available in the marketplace in which to put your money, while the return from the start-up didn't surpass what you could have achieved from these.

Failures come in all shapes and sizes. The assumption that underpins this book is that some are avoidable and some are not. If there is an end of the road, when the company is shut down, do the founders sit there and say, 'well, it seemed like a great idea, but … the market just wasn't ready for it … the technology was flawed and we could only find that out by trying to build it … the problems that arose were too difficult for us to solve, though maybe someone else will get this to work someday …' If this is an honest assessment of what happened, we can probably say these were businesses that were going to fail. I accept that such failures will represent a significant percentage of all technology start-ups.

This book is dedicated to the idea that, even after the failures that occurred for good, fundamental reasons, there remain many companies where failure was avoidable. A very few of these avoided failures will become the spectacular technology start-up successes that we read and hear about all the time, be they in software, hardware, pharmaceuticals, other biotech or agtech. We have no way of knowing which ones will be the big successes; in most cases we don't even know this after two or three years. What we do know is that if they have shut down for avoidable reasons, they will not be among them. The stories of many of the most successful technology companies include many near-death experiences, where they came within months or even weeks of having to close the company. The ideas were sound, and history proved that. What they had to do was not fail for one of the reasons I have discussed.

Most of those that don't fail because they learned the lessons in this book will provide a good if not spectacular return to the founders and the investors who backed them. Some may become public companies; many will be acquired by others at a reasonable valuation that is reflective of the hard work that went into them. The founders of these companies will also have learned a lot, about how hard it is to build a business, what their strengths and weaknesses as a leader are, how customers and competitors decide what to do in response to their offering, and how to make the ultimate decision to part with their baby now that it is somewhat grown. If we have turned 30–40 per cent of start-ups from failures to moderate success, this has also made a substantial contribution to the economy of the country or region where they have grown.

Words in a book do not keep companies from failing, any more than reading about *The Power Law* as propounded by Sebastian Mallaby ensures that 80 per cent of companies will actually fail. I have tried to lay out some causes of failure based on what I have seen and continue to see with young companies and their founders. Both the founders and the investors must be willing to ask themselves whether these ideas jibe with their own observations or teach them something that they haven't yet thought about. If they do this, and modify their behaviours and actions accordingly, there is a good chance that a lot of failures can be averted.

INDEX

accountability 89–90, 161
advanced semiconductors 144
AECOM 76
AESIN 51
AI 31, 174, 204
  generative 30
  start-up 120
Alcoa 5
alignment 128
Allen, Paul 85
aluminium 5
Amazon 4, 120, 146
Amazon Prime 146
America's Seed Fund 142
angel investors 3
  board members 107
  founders 86, 158
  fraud 28
  fundraising 132–134
  greed 121
  raising less 138–139
  venture capitalists 10, 17–18
Apple 4, 60, 120
Argonne National Laboratory 142
army 202
Asian markets 87, 145
ASPEN 92
Aspentech 92
Audit Committee 112
Automated Teller Machine (ATM) 47, 182

B2B *see* business-to-business
Baker-Hughes 50
Barclays 47
BASF 70
behavioural economics 193–200
Bertozzi, Carolyn 92

Berylls 51
Better Place 4, 148
Bezos, Jeff 96
big business, selling to 63
Board Chair, CEO mentor 130
board members
  align objectives 130
  angel investors 107
  CFO 115
  experience 130
  screw ups 22
  for show 116
boards 107–130
  actions 15
  changing the 123–125
  company leadership 108–109
  competition 115
  eliminating 125–129
  evolving 130
  governance 110–111, 130
  greed 121–122
  independent directors 115–116
  investor directors 117–120
  mentoring 122–123
  risk 111–115
  self-deception 121–122
  special events 115
  strategy 130
  tips 130
Bosch 51
BP 51
branding 188–190
Brin, Sergey 96
Builds Best Teams 103
Bulkin, Bernie 27
business 1–7
  boring 162–163
  ideas 16

INDEX

business-to-business (B2B) 46
    customers 61–62

CAC *see* customer acquisition cost
Cambridge 75
capital costs 47, 72
capital gains 11
care homes 49
cars 77–78
cash flow 95–96, 99–100
    shortages 135–137
Catholic Church 202
CBInsights 110
CFO *see* Chief Financial Officer
Chaplin, Charlie 34
ChatGPT 150, 191
Chemical Bank 47
Chief Financial Officer (CFO) 136–137
    board members 115
    employees 205
    fraud 90
    governance 111
    government funding 151
    growth 94
    hiring 106
    leadership 98–100, 103
    mentoring 109, 123, 130
Chief Technology Officer (CTO) 55, 85–86, 97–98, 103, 106, 203
Citibank 47
Cleantech 2, 39, 51–52, 54
Climate 51–52
CNRS France 142
coal mining waste 33–34
Coca-Cola 189
Coke 188
competencies 102
    self-assessment 106
competition 39, 178–179
    boards 115
competitive barriers 35–36
competitors, switching cost 63
computers 78
contract engineering partners 82

conversion rates 197
cornered resources 180–181
cost switching 63, 185–187
Costco 188
costs
    customers 60, 77, 185–188
    fuel 37
    goods 146
counter-positioning 181–183
Covid vaccines 15
CRISPR 29
crowdfunding 17–18, 132
CTO *see* Chief Technology Officer
cues, visual 199
customer acquisition cost (CAC) 49, 59, 186, 197
customers
    B2B 61–62
    board members 126
    brands 188–190
    costs 60, 77, 185–188
    deceiving 133
    delivery 67–68, 78, 82
    educating 54–55, 160
    field testing 161–162
    fraud 28
    influential 60, 76, 114, 123
    markets 45–50, 57
    payments from 146
    potential 32, 58–59, 63, 137, 191, 196–197
    problems 181
    reaching 48, 198–200, 208
    relationships 150
    retaining 182–184
    risks 129
    selling to 145
    targeting 15, 20
    understanding 171
cybersecurity 61, 112

de Geus, Arie 193, 200–201
debt funding 153
delegation degree 161–162

INDEX

delivery, customers 67–68, 78, 82
Denso 51
Development Bank Wales 132
diapers, disposable 32
dishonesty 110
Doerr, John 67, 171
dominant design 15, 162–163
Drucker, Peter 204
Duke Energy 61
DuPont 65, 70

economics, behavioural 193–200
economies
    network 187–188
    scale 183–185
Edison, Thomas 5, 58, 85, 98
Eisenhower, Dwight D. 178
Eisenmann, Tom 23
electric light 58
electric vehicles 54, 66, 117, 173, 182
electrical components 79
electrical devices 85
electrical engineers 29, 70–71, 73
electricity
    capacity 48
    processing power 30–31, 79
    provision 49, 85, 165
    scale-up 34–35
    waste conversion 54
Eli Lilly (Mounjaro) 60
employees
    board members 126, 192
    Chief Financial Officer (CFO) 205
    dishonesty 110
    engineers 77–81
    managing 99, 159, 171–172, 191
    satisfaction 16, 201
    shareholders 11, 19, 111, 121
    training 185
    turnover 14, 96, 205
engineers 65–66
    contract 75
    disciplines 71–73

electrical 29, 70–71, 73
employing 77–81
engineering 67–69
    in-house 76–77
    out-of-house 75–77
problem solving 69–71
quality 73–75
tips 82
entrepreneurs 5–6, 14–15, 17–18, 21
    encouraging 141
    engineering 67–69, 72–73, 75
    expanding 157–158
    flawed technology 29–30, 36–37, 40–42
    leadership 85
    markets 45, 50, 53–54, 56–57
    patents 164
    and venture firms 138
Erasmus University 193
ethics 199–200
    presentations 42
Evans, Larry 92
Exxon 51, 61

FAANG *see* Facebook, Amazon, Apple, Netflix, Google
Facebook, Amazon, Apple, Netflix, Google (FAANG) 120
Facebook/Meta 4, 12, 59, 120, 122, 178, 187
failure
    causes of 19–23
    see also individual causes
Fast Tomatoes 57
Fastspin Company 27–28
fear of missing out (FOMO) 42
field testing 161–162
financial irregularities 98–99
Firelake Capital Management 147–148
focus 155–157
follow-on money 18
FOMO *see* fear of missing out
Forbes magazine 67
Ford 51, 61, 66

founders 80
    angel investors 86, 158
    arrogant 87–88
    leadership 84–89, 97–98
Four Seasons 188
fraud
    angel investors 28
    Chief Financial Officer (CFO) 90
    customers 28
    technical experts 42
Freedom to Operate 164
fuel 47, 190
    biofuel 173
    costs 37
    products 20, 27, 33, 40, 65
fuel cells 144
fundraising
    angel investors 132–134
    money 132–133, 137–139
    multiple rounds 153
funds
    siphoning off 89–90
    venture capital 6, 9–10, 12, 19, 39, 120

Gates, Bill 85
Gekko, Gordon 122
Genentech 4
General Electric 178
General Motors 66
General Partner (GP) 10–11, 18
generative AI 30
GM 51
Goldilocks problems 140
Google 15, 60, 120
governance 109–111, 118
    boards 110–111, 130
government
    funding 17, 100, 132, 141–145, 151, 153
    partners 51–53
GP *see* General Partner
greed
    angel investors 121
    boards 121–122
Green Angel Syndicate 3

Green Angel Ventures 3
greenhouse gases 54
Greenspan, Alan 14
growth 94

Haliburton 50–51
Hall, Charles Martin 5
Hanergy 148
Headspin 26
Helmer, Hamilton, *7 Powers* 170, 179–180, 182, 190–193
Hermes 188
Hilton 188
hiring 82
Hot Tomatoes 57
House of Lords 26–27
Huang, Jensen 167, 203
hydrogen 30
hydrogen fuel cells 144
hype cycle, investments 42

Ikea 20, 131
income tax 11
independent directors 115–116
initial public offering (IPO) 10, 12, 14, 119–120, 140
intellectual property (IP) 4, 163–166
    patents 40, 180–181
    protecting 135–136
    selling 157
    valuing 189
Intellectual Property Portfolio 166
Internal Rate of Return (IRR) 12
international expansion 157
inventors 5, 26, 78, 83–84
investment
    effective 174–177
    efficient 172–174
    venture capital 138, 147
    venture capital firms 177
investors
    board directors 117–120
    potential 26, 68, 80, 134, 137, 150, 176
    venture capitalists 3–4, 10, 17–18

involvement degree 161–162
IP *see* intellectual property
IPO *see* initial public offering
IQ 87
IRR *see* Internal Rate of Return

Jacobs 76
Jawbone 4
Job, Book of 52
Johnson, Boris 30–31

Kahneman, Daniel 171, 196
   Thinking Fast and Slow 194
Kamprad, Ingvar 131
Kennedy, John F. 178
Kleiner Perkins Caufield & Byers 147
know-how 180
Kodak 182

Langer, Robert 92
large learning models 144
Lawrence Livermore National Laboratory 141–142
leadership 15, 22, 83–106
   and boards 108–109
   Chief Financial Officer 98–100, 103
   commitment 92–93
   entrepreneurs 85
   external 96–97
   founders 84–89, 97–98
   growth of 93–96
   improving 100–105
   lifestyle 90–91
   media star CEO 88–89
   misuse of 89–90
   money raising person as CEO 86–87
   most arrogant person as CEO 87–88
   tech person as CEO 85–86
   tips 106
leadership team 82
leads change 201
Lean Startup, The (Ries) 45
Lily Robotics 26, 28
Limited Partners (LP) 10–11, 18, 39

LinkedIn 187
location, in technological cluster 82
London Stock Exchange 91
long-term value (LTV) 49, 166, 186, 190
Los Alamos National Laboratory 141
Louis Vuitton 188
LP *see* Limited Partners
LTV *see* long-term value
Ludgate Investments 3

Magma 51
Mallaby, Sebastian 13, 208
marketing 159–160
markets
   Asian 87, 145
   competition 57–58
   customers 45–50, 57
   dealing with 58–62
   educating 46–48
   entrepreneurs 45, 50, 53–54, 56–57
   gaps 53–57
   government partners 51–53
   players 63
   tips 63
   understanding 15, 22, 63
mass manufacture 77–78
mass market 47, 156
MathWorks 20, 186
MATLAB 186
Medium 166
mentoring
   boards 122–123
   CFO 109, 123, 130
Mercedes 51
Meta/Facebook 4, 12, 59, 120, 122, 178, 187
MiaSolé 147–148
Micawber Principle 145
Microsoft 131
MIT 92
Modern Times 34
money 131–153
   analysis of 133–134
   cash shortages 135–137
   correct provision of 149–152

fundraising 132–133, 137–139
government 141–145
investments 147–149
sufficient 15, 134–135
tips 153
valuation 139–141
working capital 145–147
mRNA vaccines 173
Munger, Charlie 87

nappies, disposable 32
Netflix 12, 120
network economies 187–188
Nikola 26
Nobel Prize 92
Nvidia 167, 203

Oak Ridge National Laboratory 141
observers 107
Outcome Health 26

Papoulis, Athanasios 73
partners
    venture capital 10, 12, 23, 86, 91, 125
    venture capital firms 40, 87
patents 27, 88, 92, 136
    entrepreneurs 164
    intellectual property (IP) 40, 164–166, 180–181
paths, successful 169–172, 204–206
    behavioural economics 193–200
    branding 188–190
    conversion rates 197
    cornered resources 180–181
    cost switching 185–187
    counter-positioning 181–183
    effective investment 174–177
    efficient investment 172–174
    ethics 199–200
    network economies 187–188
    people 200–204
    process power 190–191
    products 197–198
    scale economies 183–185
    strategy 177–193
    structure 200–204
    testing 200
    urgency 198
    users 196–200
    visual cues 199
PayCoin 26, 28
payments, customers 146
people, paths to 200–204
Pepsi 188
pharmaceuticals 14–15
Pittsburgh Reduction Company 5
Ponzi scheme 28
Porter, Michael 53, 79, 177–178
post money valuation 121
potential customers 32, 58–59, 63, 137, 191, 196–197
Power Law, The 208
pre-money valuation 18, 139
presentations, ethical 42
process power 190–191
product engineering 15
products 197–198

Qatar of Hydrogen 30
quantum computing 144
questions, outset 42

relationships, customers 150
reliability 15, 50, 68–69, 76–78, 82, 142
resources, cornered 180–181
Ries, Eric, *The Lean Startup* 45
Right Path, The 171
risk
    boards 111–115
    customers 129
    understanding 166–167
Ritz Carlton 188
rock star founders 56
Rockefeller, John D. 202
Rothschilds 158
Royal Society of Arts 193
rules 21, 60, 99, 127, 140
Rumsfeld, Donald 6

S&P 500 tracker fund 9
Sales/Marketing 103
scale economies 183–185
scale-up 20, 22, 41, 59, 66, 69
    risk 25, 31–35
Scottish Enterprise 132
seed funding 17
seed patents 92
seeding 2
    America's Seed Fund 142
self-deception, boards 121–122
7 Powers (Helmer) 170, 179–180, 182, 190–193
shareholders 84, 89, 112, 126, 151
    employees 11, 19, 111, 121
shares 18–19, 116, 148
Shell 50–51, 194
Silicon Valley 66–67
    arrogance 68
    failures 56, 66
    grand slams 13
    Paul Thiel 4
    venture capital 20, 36, 118
skills
    developing 102–104
    gaps 106
SLB 50
solar energy 163, 182
    cells 34–35, 147
    farms 23, 52, 163
    material 35
    modules 147
    photovoltaics 35
staff, loss of 96
Standard Oil 202
Stanford 92
Starbucks 189
start-ups
    funding 16–19, 153
    leadership evolution 106
Strategic Conceptualizer 103
Strategic Influencer 103
Strategic Partners *see* Limited Partners
strategy, successful 177–193

Strengths, Weaknesses, Opportunities and Threats (SWOT) 178
structure, successful 200–204
success, evaluating 207–209
Sunstein, Cass 171, 195–196
Swan, Joseph 98
SWOT *see* Strengths, Weaknesses, Opportunities and Threats
System 1 194–195, 198
System 2 194–195, 198

Taiwan, Government of 53
Taiwan Semiconductor Manufacturing Company (TSMC) 53, 189
TAM *see* total available market
team building 103
technical support 49, 185
technology 25–42
    at scale 42
    competition barriers 35–36
    flawed premises 29–31
    fraud 26–29
    improvement limits 36–37
    real 37–41
    scale-up risk 31–35
    tips 42
Tesla 4, 12, 54
testing 161–162, 200
Thaler, Richard 171, 195–196
Theranos 26
Thiel, Peter 4
Thinking Fast and Slow (Kahneman) 194
Tier 1 suppliers 50–51, 61, 199
Tier 2 suppliers 51, 189, 199
Tier 3 suppliers 51
Tiffany 188
timidity 22
total available market (TAM) 45
training, employees 185
TSMC *see* Taiwan Semiconductor Manufacturing Company
turnover, employees 14, 96, 205
Twitter 187